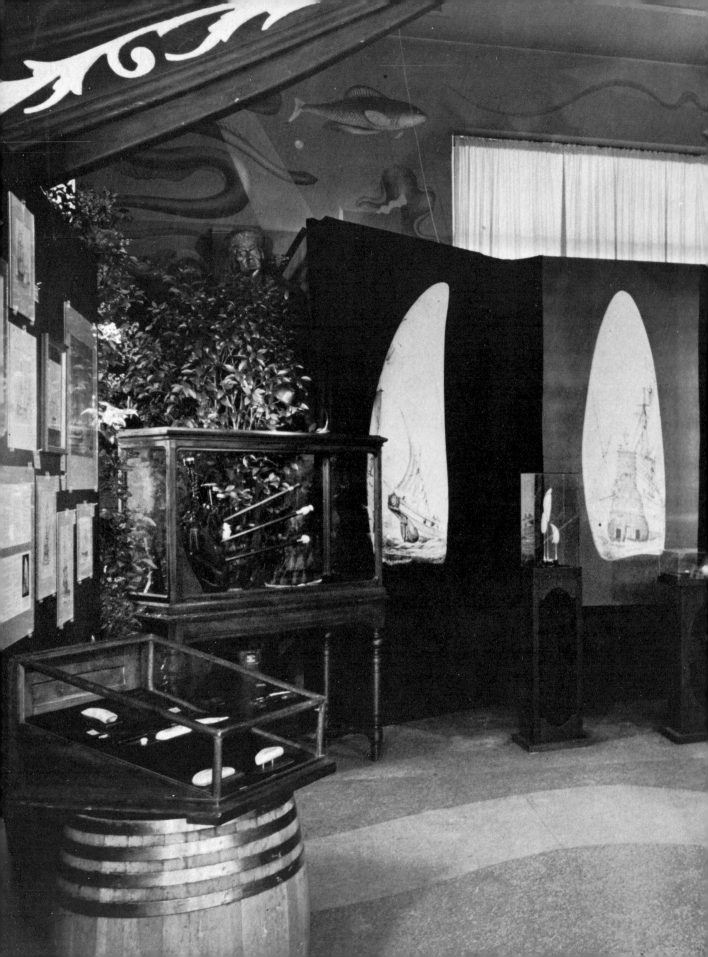

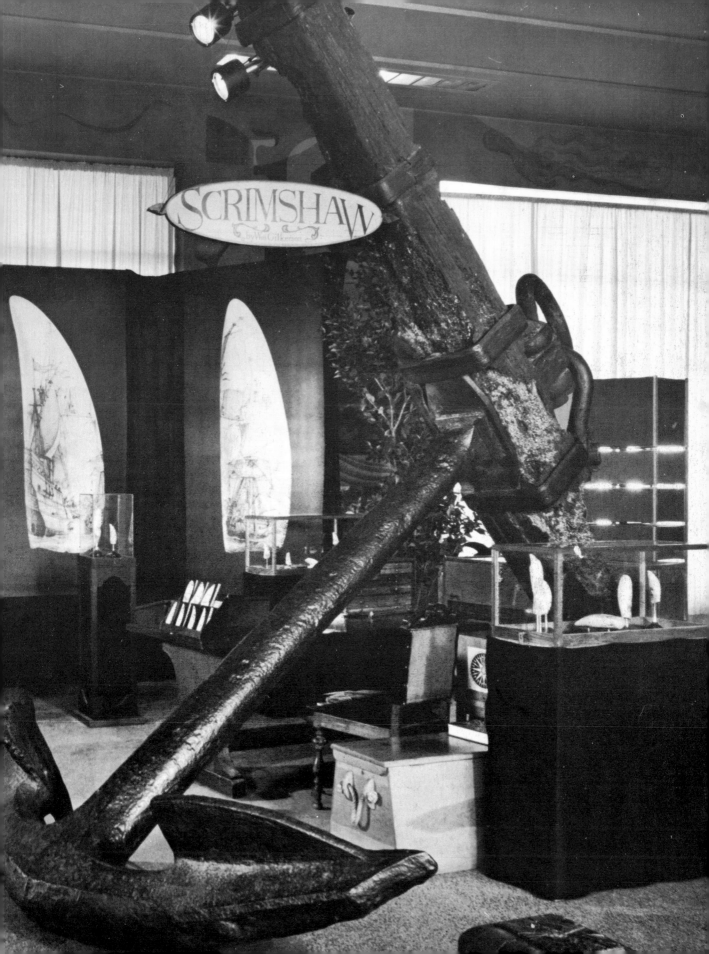

Scrimshawing, making dippers and picture frames. Making jagging irons. Feel rather disheartened. Home looks distant. My mind still will wander homewards . . . I can almost jump overboard. Scrimshawing . . .

Sold a cane to the mate of an English brig . . . The end of 1871 is fast approaching, also is eternity . . .

Scrimshawing . . .

Journal of John Coquin,
bark Globe, *Coast of*
Africa, 1871

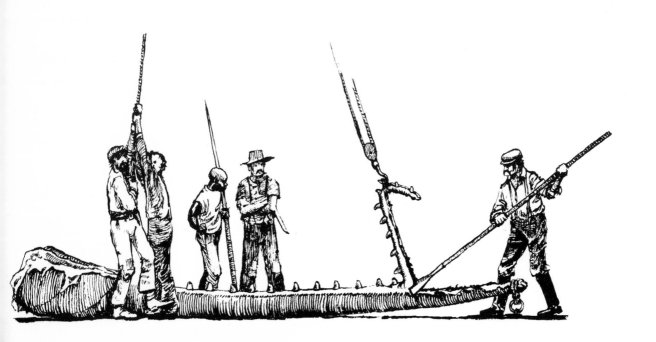

The SCRIMSHANDER

by

William Gilkerson

with

introduction by

Karl Kortum

Troubador Press San Francisco

PUBLISHER'S NOTE: *The pieces of scrimshaw appearing in this book have for the most part been reproduced as close to actual size as possible. Notable exceptions are reduction of some of the larger artifacts, or the older pieces, and the details, which greatly magnify the originals. Materials unidentified by captions or text include all the brush and ink illustrations throughout, which are the author's work, as is the cover piece. The double page photograph appearing before the title page shows the recent special exhibit of work by the author in the main hall of the San Francisco Maritime Museum.*

Library of Congress Catalog Number: 74-24008
ISBN: 0-912300-53-1 (Paperbound) ISBN: 0-912300-54-X (Hardbound)

Contents

Introduction by Karl Kortum 2

I   Scrimshaw: The Old 5

II   Scrimshaw: The New 22

III   An Endangered Species,
An Endangered Art Form 36

Chapters IV through IX are a
Photographic Portfolio of Scrimshaw
by the author

IV   Whalers 42

V   Ship Portraits 53

VI   The Crafted Artifact 75

VII   Fantasy and Imagery 84

VIII Pirates 96

IX   Tools and Techniques 104

Acknowledgements 114

Bibliography 116

Index 117

Introduction

Once in a while, out of the woods of Mendocino, emerges a watery figure by the name of Bill Gilkerson. With gleaming eye and short black beard, he makes his way to San Francisco. He may get here by Greyhound bus, but I doubt it — some kind of levitation seems more likely. Hanging at his side is a cowhide bag, and inside the bag are pouches, each holding a piece of scrimshaw.

Illustrations of those pieces are assembled in this book for the first time. They speak for themselves as an extension of an American folk art into new beauties and subtleties. In this book they are cumulative, but we have had the privilege of seeing them emerge one at a time over the years out of the cowhide wallet. The effect is like the arrival in town of some Renaissance artisan, some transient Cellini, displaying mesmerically his year's production of curiosities worked in whale ivory.

When I use the term "watery" for Gilkerson, I mean he has the water-sense as defined by Cyril Ionides in *A Floating Home:* "In many people the sight of water responds to some fundamental need of the mind. To the vision of these disciples of Thales everything that is agreeable somehow proceeds from water, and into water everything may somehow be resolved. When they are away from water they are vaguely uncomfortable, perhaps feeling that the road to freedom and escape is cut off. Inland they will walk, like Shelley, across a field to look at trickling water in a ditch, or will search out a dirty canal in the midst of an industrial town. The sea, which to some eyes seems to lead nowhere, seems to them to lead everywhere."

William Gilkerson went to sea at the age of fourteen, shipping as messboy on the Norwegian freighter *Ringvilde* at New Orleans. The *Ringvilde* carried sheet steel to Ecuador, and returned with bananas. It is an old tradition; the Baltic seafaring peoples believe in an early start and a hardening process for the boys on their ships. Bill passed through the Panama Canal four times before he was allowed out on deck to look at it.

Gilkerson's first vessel of his own was a run-down ex-royal yacht which he bought in Norway in 1961. This was the fifty-foot cutter *Kalliope* built in 1896 for King Christian IX of Denmark. The price was $1,250 and the king's yacht was in deplorable condition. Gilkerson restored the *Kalliope* and sailed her around the Baltic, the North Sea, and the English Channel. In the south of England he re-rigged the vessel into a ketch, cutting the trees for mast and spars himself.

Our scrimshander (although he had not yet found his art) returned to the United States and wrote and illustrated a book, *Gilkerson on War,* a satirical treatment of the military history of mankind, then went to work as a writer and editor for the *San Francisco Chronicle.* Living aboard his Hannah-design Carol Ketch, *Griffyn,* he worked and cruised the California coast.

Around that time, a bartender in North Beach gave Gilkerson a pristine whale's tooth which he was moved to engrave with the new scrimshaw. That started him off.

I first met Bill during these years; he anchored the *Griffyn* in the lagoon in front of the Maritime Museum one evening and came ashore to pick up my son Johnny and myself. The cabin lights glowed in the gray-blue twilight as we clambered aboard; Bill subsequently engraved the scene on a whale's tooth for me (page 70).

There seems to be an effort by some scrimshaw collectors to limit the term "scrimshaw" to the products of the last century, more or less. They are rightly concerned with imitations of the old scrimshaw elbowing into the market place and diluting the verity and importance of the real thing. The best that can be hoped for, it seems to me, are definitions of "old scrimshaw," "new scrimshaw," and "imitation old scrimshaw." Gilkerson is unabashedly a new scrimshaw man.

I have some idea, from experience, of why the old stuff was created. The Second Assistant Engineer, Geoffrey Baskerville, of the motorship *Lorinna* or the steamer *San Antonio* (I forget just which, now; we served in both vessels) had a large pearl shell, about eight inches across. The ship was lying in one of those palm-girt harbors on the north coast of New Guinea, tediously unloading military cargo in World War II.

Leaning over the rail and gabbing with our shipmates wore itself out as pastime. I suggested to Geof that he turn the piece of pearl shell into a work of art with a fret saw. He asked me what I meant, and I drew a scene for him right across it, complete with drooping palm tree. Glad to have something to kill time, Geof went below and spent many hours cutting out and polishing the scene.

Boredom – the mate of the *Acushnet* must have been out of whale teeth when he entered in the log on December 16, 1845: "Busy doing nothing–nothing to do it with."

When Geof's work was done, it was the envy of his shipmates. Moreover, it was true to the scrimshaw tradition because what Geof really had in mind was giving it to his girl in Sydney, Australia when the voyage was done.

Walter Earle, curator of the Cold Spring Harbor Whaling Museum, describes why boredom found a special home on a whaling ship:

". . . Twenty-four was the minimum crew for the smallest cruising whaling vessel, be it schooner or brig. That meant at least twenty-four rugged sailors to feed and keep, for from two to four years at a single stretch, cooped up in a small vessel. Of course, they had other duties and chores in addition to taking and processing whales . . . But all such routine chores, all the shipkeeping that the most exacting master could devise were little indeed for a crew of twenty-five in a vessel, which, in any other use, would be adequately manned and operated by six, or perhaps eight, men."

The old scrimshaw was an escape from the sea – from too much sea – back towards the land. The new scrimshaw moves in the other direction.

Karl Kortum
Director
San Francisco
Maritime Museum

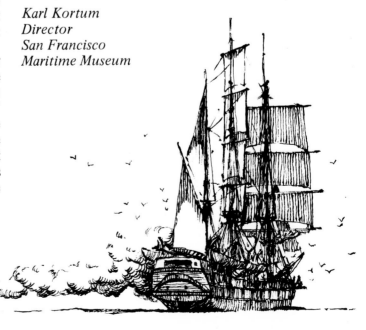

A SCRIMSHANDER and a scrimshaw collector, both from the last century, are illustrated in these two vintage photographs. Right — the young scrimshander poses dockside with his materials, the jawbone of a sperm whale and its teeth, one of which he is scraping smooth with his knife. Below — Abe Warner, one of San Francisco's historical eccentrics, stands at the bar of his famed Cobweb Palace, a North Beach saloon built just after the gold rush. It was so named because of his refusal to dust. Warner held the conviction spiders had as much right to the place as did he, so cobwebs festooned rafters, walls and even the walrus tusks and whale teeth of his scrimshaw collection, acquired from sailors for drinks. Amongst the scrimshaw, a big red parrot preened, screeching: "I'll have a rum and gum! What'll you have?"

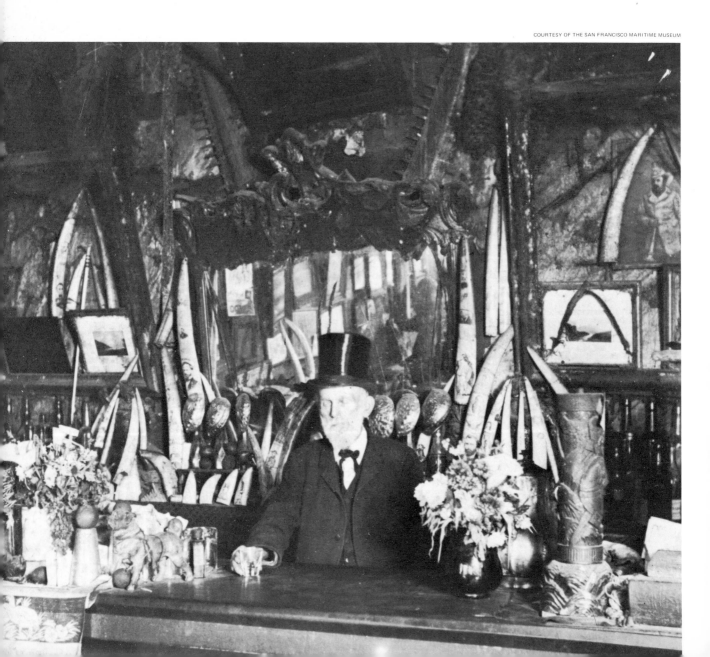

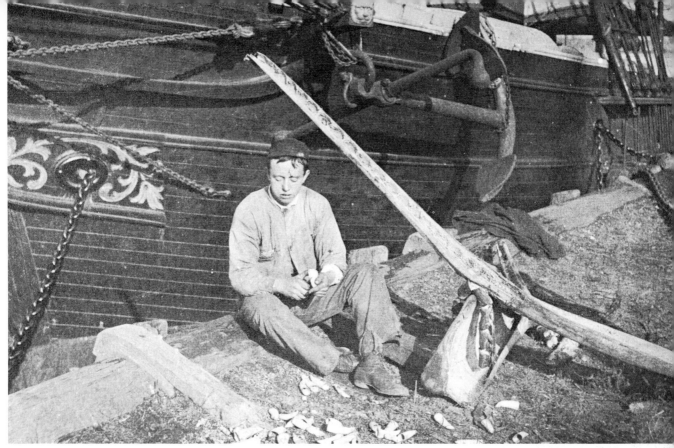

I Scrimshaw: The Old

Let us walk through the cool clean corridors of a whaling museum, where we can still see the tools of that now extinct era of wooden ships; the irons — harpoons, lances, cutting spades, boarding knives — all neatly arrayed in fan pattern against their display board. They are black and pitted and lethal looking, but at the same time curiously harmless in this hushed setting. The viewer gets the same feeling from them somehow as from an old cannon in a park, its barrel stuffed with popcorn boxes and birds' nests. Here are the irons, wired securely in place, carefully labeled, themselves their own monuments. The information placard tells us one New Bedford smithy alone made 77,000 harpoons.

And over here is a whaleboat, fully found and fitted, all her gear aboard, rudder shipped, steering sweep and oars in place. Her line tubs are full of meticulously coiled manila ready to attach to the harpoon and pay out smoking around the loggerhead, attaching this fragile boat to its destiny, the plunging black fury of the giant whale. Near the place where the harpooner stands is his hatchet, so this line may be cut if there's an emergency. Here too is the mast, sail and rigging in place. Everything is ready to the last detail, all the bits; grappling hook, compass, bucket, piggin, water keg. The keg is empty, of course, as dry as the bones of the sailors who last used this gear in pursuit of a whale.

Children run clattering and giggling through the halls, their cries echoing. They are told to behave themselves by the lady at the gift counter where pamphlets and books are sold along with little anchors, tiny ships in bottles and other such items.

"Please, children, this is a museum! Quiet! Quiet!"

We stroll on, past the paintings and models of the old ships. The yards of the models are tautly braced, squarer and more symmetrical than ever they were in real life, stripped of their sails. And here are table-cases containing yellowed journals and logs with brief but eloquent entries:

"Dusty times, I tell you . . . Strange works and strange times, I assure you . . . Hard old times . . . the old man and the Mate had a growl . . . Easy time now. The old

man and the mate are on good terms, but I guess it wont last long."
(Log of the *John Bunyan,* off Greenland)

It is so easy to romanticize U.S. whaling today, now that it is dead and the harpoons are wired to walls and the boats are on concrete chocks, and nobody can smell it any more. That smell was infamous, and if one trace of it was to manifest in these halls, it would be attacked at once with fumigation equipment.

We arrive at cases containing dozens and dozens of etched whale teeth and carved artifacts. Scrimshaw. The art of the yankee whalerman. No whaling museum is complete without this display. Since it is our special interest, let us stop here, where the information card tells us that, according to some old accounts, there were times when whales were sighted by crewmen who were so involved in their scrimshaw work they kept quiet about the whales.

NAVAL BATTLE between John Paul Jones' flagship BonHomme Richard *and British* Serapis, *depicted on the tooth below, probably from the early 19th century, has long been a favorite for scrimshanders. A recent version of the action appears on front and back covers.*

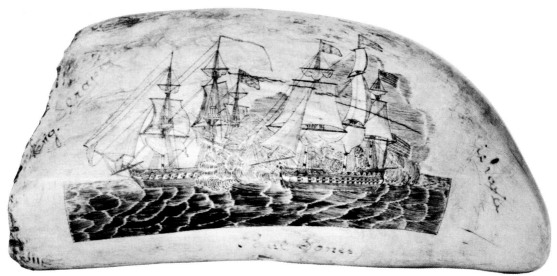

Most of the teeth in the case are cracked and orange with age, covered with miniature engraving, for the most part rather crude. Some of the artifacts are recognizable objects — canes, knives, rings and such — but some are puzzling to our modern eye.

What is scrimshaw?

Those who have ·written on the subject have yet to come up with two definitions that are the same, but the narrowest views are generally held by directors of whaling museums. One such director recently interviewed offered the following:

"Scrimshaw was done by whalermen of the last century, or before, on whale ships, on whaling voyages, using a variety of materials, mostly parts of the whale. It is not a present-day activity because there is no more whaling."

He was questioned on this. What about work done by other sailors, from the sailing navy or merchant marine, for instance?

"Unless it was done by whalermen it is not scrimshaw."

Well, what about relatively recent work done aboard the whale ships of this century?

"If it was done aboard a whale ship, it would be within the definition."

How about work done ashore by retired whalermen? The distinguished looking gentleman considered this question for a moment. "Under those circumstances it would be authentic if done in the last century."

And if a retired whalerman did scrimshaw work ashore in this century?

"No. It would not be within the definition. It would have to have been done by the end of the last century, and by the water."

You mean, before the year 1900, exactly?

"Yes." A wave of the hand. "There has

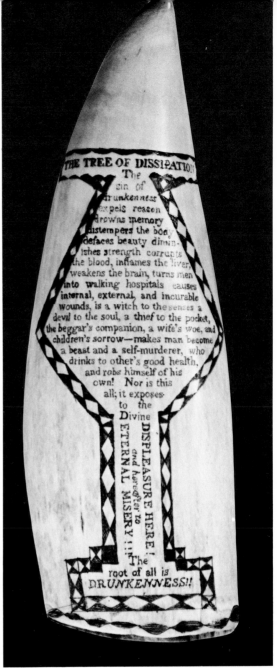

"TREE OF DISSIPATION" — *A very early, anonymous scrimshaw'd tooth warns: "The sin of drunkenness expels reason, drowns memory, distempers the body, defaces beauty, diminishes strength, corrupts the blood, inflames the liver, weakens the brain, turns men into walking hospitals, causes internal, external and incurable wounds . . ."*

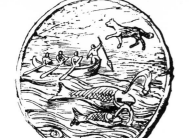

to be some line drawn in this kind of thing." A slight frown. "I realize this sounds rather narrow . . ."

Most nautical authorities, especially those not devoted quite so exclusively to whaling, feel that while the art of scrimshaw was undeniably born on whale ships, it spread into wide nautical use and survived the death of the whaling industry. The more-or-less generally accepted definition is summed up by Norman Flayderman in his encyclopedic *Scrimshaw and Scrimshanders,* a book to which students of scrimshaw are directed. It is the most extensive work on the subject of antique scrimshaw yet done. Quoth Mr. Flayderman:

Scrimshaw is ". . . the art of carving or otherwise fashioning useful or decorative articles as practiced primarily by whalermen, sailors, or others associated with nautical pursuits. The basic materials of the artifacts are from the whale. Other materials may be taken from various forms of sea life, shells, or diverse materials gathered in areas visited by ships, as well as woods, metals, etc. normally carried or used aboard ships. The artifacts must have a nautical association in respect to one or more of the following: maker, motif, method, or materials."

We glance again into the glass case. The whale teeth are still there, apparently unchanged. None have tumbled from their shelf.

Some 40 years ago whaling historian Clifford Ashley authored a book called *The Yankee Whaler.* Although now out of print, it was long considered a definitive text, and in it Ashley called scrimshaw " . . . The

only important indigenous folk art, except that of the Indians, we have ever had in America."

Ashley has been often quoted and defended on this by some, and attacked by others. The answer seems to be that both sides are right, and the controversy has existed because the word *scrimshaw* denotes two distinctly separate categories of work, each with a different continent of origin.

Scrimshaw includes a variety of crafted artifacts, such as canes, work boxes, busks, etc. (see page 12), which all together form one category. The second category of scrimshaw includes only engraved ivory—primarily the teeth of sperm whales, and it is this work which American whalermen originated and refined into a folk art, perhaps indeed North America's only indigenous, non-aboriginal art.

As for the former category, American sailors did much of the crafted work also, but it originated in Europe, where whalermen who had never seen a sperm whale were fashioning articles from the bones of baleen whales long before the colonization of North America.

While scrimshaw as an art form is no longer the property of the whaling industry, it was sired by it, and so the stories of scrimshaw and whaling entwine. Melville offers Perseus as the first whaleman, killing a whale which was on the verge of eating the Ethiopian Princess Andromeda. There are various biblical references to whale hunting, and many primitive peoples have whaled since time before memory. Among some South Sea islanders, whale teeth are used as cash currency.

The Indians who inhabited Nantucket were whalermen centuries before the arrival

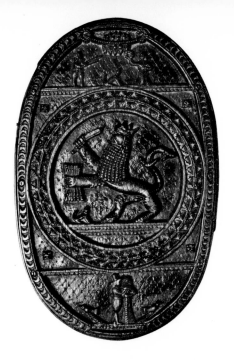

CAP BOX made aboard a Dutch whaler dates to early 17th century; actual size: eight inches wide, 12 long, five high.

of the white people, who themselves had whaling ancestors in far northern waters long before Christ.

Historian M. V. Brewington mentions having seen a rock carving in Sweden depicting an oar-propelled boat containing men, one in the bow with a spear, obviously pursuing a whale, which has been dated circa 3500 B.C.

The first organized whaling industry as such seems to have originated with the Basques in Medieval times. They were fishing the Bay of Biscay around 1000 A.D. and later expanded their range of operations northward and westward, to Spitzbergen and Newfoundland. In the Allan Forbes Whaling Collection at the Massachusetts Institute of Technology, there is the small seal of a Basque town of around 1400 A.D. showing a chase after whales from a small boat. It is a remarkably scrimshaw-like object.

Possibly the earliest piece of actual shipboard scrimshaw work extant is from Holland. The Dutch fished for baleen whales in the far northern waters of the Atlantic from 1600 until the mid 1700's. Their peak years were between 1699 and 1708, during which time 1,652 ships sailed from Dutch ports. The lamps of Europe burned with Dutch whale oil taken among the ice floes of Greenland and Jan Mayen Land, although the British and the French also had sizable whaling fleets.

The Dutch scrimshaw mentioned is a cap box brought from The Netherlands by Brewington for the Kendall collection. It was one of two pieces which were very much alike and obviously of the same period. The companion piece was dated 1631.

The Kendall's box has a top of dark wood, deeply carved with patterns, small figures and a royal lion, rampant. Its sides are etched with profile depictions of Dutch whaling ships (fluyts) of the mid-1600's. The sides are made of baleen. Baleen is the springy, grey-green, brown or black fibrous substance which is found in the mouths of all large whales except the Sperm Whale, which has teeth. Baleen plates make strainers through which the whale's food is trapped. Among Yankee whalermen it was called whalebone, though it is not bone as such.

Scrimshaw from The Netherlands is rare, and, judging from the amount that still exists, the Dutch whalermen did not do very much. Possibly in the ice fields of the polar seas their fingers were too stiff.

In warmer waters, a century or so later, the art began to flourish, and when it did, it was at the hands of Americans.

Sometime in 1712, Captain Christopher Hussey and his crew were fishing for baleen whales in a small sloop out of Nantucket, when a sudden hard wind blew them further offshore than they had intended to go. There, in deeper water and howling wind, they found themselves in the midst of a pack of whales — sperm whales, not the baleen whales they were used to taking closer to shore.

Wind or no wind, here were whales. Over went a boat, a whale was attacked and killed, and then the sloop sheltered out the blow in the lee of the giant corpse. When conditions grew calmer, they stripped it of blubber and returned to Nantucket with a higher quality of whale oil than any of the baleen whales produced.

Until that moment, the spermaceti whale had been safe from the harpoons of the colonists. He cruised in deeper waters than his cousins, in search of the shoals of squid with which he satisfied his considerable appetite. Instead of baleen, he had teeth in his lower jaw which fit into corresponding sockets in the upper jaw when his mouth closed. Page 11 shows a sperm whale lying on his back next to the whale ship as his mighty jaw, pulled open with tackles, is removed with cutting spades.

In those jaws he could easily crush the dainty hull of a whaleboat, it was soon learned. He was found to be a tougher customer than the Nantucketers were used to, but his discovery meant the birth of the Yankee offshore whale fishery. It also meant a new-found supply of soft, rich ivory teeth, ivory with a marbled pattern, unlike any of the other kinds of ivory. These teeth could be carved, slabbed or engraved with delicate, minature patterns.

Sperm whales were thereafter pursued by many small vessels, some no bigger than medium-sized offshore sailing yachts of today. When they made a catch, they would stow the blubber and return to port, where it would be rendered into oil. When the whales began avoiding the shore by ever-increasing distances, bigger vessels were built to range in pursuit.

These came to be rigged with tryworks — furnaces with iron kettles to *try* the blubber, to boil out its oil, for stowage in casks carried aboard. This system allowed even longer voyages, and by the end of the 1700's the Yankee whalers were ranging around Cape Horn and into the Pacific.

As cruises continued to increase in duration, a two or three-year voyage came to be commonplace and one of four or five years was accepted by crews as a possibility. The longest whaling voyage on record is probably that of *Nile* of New London, which made a cruise lasting from 1858 to 1869.

It was on voyages such as these that the art of scrimshaw flowered. We can match the articles in their glass case with entries in the old journals:

"Making granny's Scratcher."

"Getting out some whale bone to make a cane for Dr. Winslow."

"The Cooper is making whalebone brooms."

And in the journal of Gurdon Hall, aboard the whaler *Charles Phelps* in 1844, we read:

"The Captain, officers, Boatsteerers and foremast hands Busily employed sawing up Bones for Canes, Swifts, Busks, fids, Gilmet and chisel handles, etc."

This was scrimshaw, an endless list of things, some useful, some useless, big and little, limited only by the imagination or available material. A list of items of scrimshaw appears in the caption, page 12, an illustration of an elaborate jagging wheel. Jagging wheels were favored items to make, as were corset busks (see page 13), presents

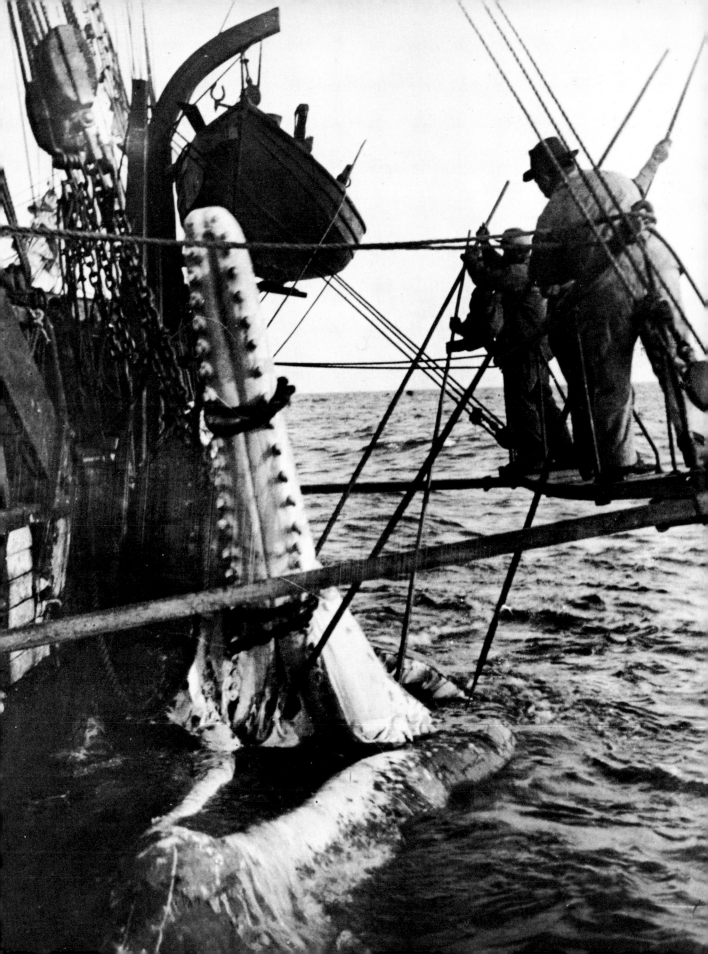

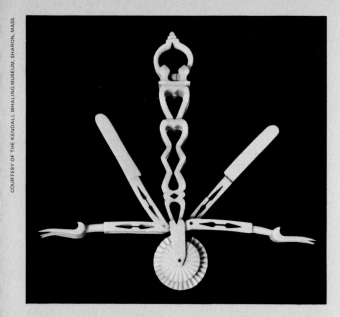

THE JAGGING WHEEL was a traditionally favorite artifact for the scrimshander's hand. Made of bone or ivory, it was for the lady back home who would hopefully celebrate the gift by making a big, juicy pie. The wheel crimped the crust, the tines pierced it to emit steam, the blade cut it. The above example is like a Swiss Army Knife of jagging wheels, with two of each tool, all folding.

The imagination was the only limit to items created under the scrimshaw label. One sailor scrimshaw'd the entire front part of his house, plus a fence, by working on the bits at sea, putting them in place between voyages.

Yankee whaler Clifford Ashley lists implements created: "Bird-cages, baskets, work-boxes, checker-boards and dominoes, chessmen and jackstraws, swifts and parrels, busks and stays, bodkins and knitting needles, tool-handles and rolling pins, clothes-pins and dish mops, rings and bracelets, salt shakers and napkin rings, canes and whips, jig blocks and belaying pins, coat racks and embroidery frames, writing desks and boxes, cribbage boards and work tables, brackets and frames, rulers, penholders, paper knives, brushes, butterspreaders, cuff links, scarf ornaments, fids, scribers, seam rubbers, spool racks, needle cases, card trays, sleds, baby wagons, foot scrapers, door stops, hooks, knobs and hinges."

To this can be added: tie pins and tacks, necklaces and earrings, toys and dolls, model ships and cups, key chains and charms, belt buckles and beckets, thimbles, plumb bobs, stash bottles, pistol grips, flag halliard cleats and alphabet plaques, fiddle pegs, half-hulls, folding fans, fobs and fipple whistles.

for the ladies back home.

Everybody scrimshaw'd, from the captain on down. From the log of the bark *Benjamin Cummings,* dated New Year's day, 1858, we read:

"Captain Jenkins and wife and all hands scrimshoring."

So even the lady folk scrimshaw'd. Or scrimshored. The word is noted with many spellings.

"Finished my scrimshoning and stowed away my tools."

Other variations include skrimshanding, scromschonting, scrimpschoning, schrimson, scrimsharn, scrimshorn, schrimpshong, skrimshonting, skimshontering, squimshon, skrumpshunk and crackjaw.

"Scrimshaw" seems to have been settled on as the common denominator of a word the origins of which are even more obscure than its definition. These elusive beginnings have been pursued to right scholarly lengths by some writers about the art, but none conclusively.

Old Yankee Ashley thinks *scrim* comes from the old Yankee word *scrimp,* because scrimping or economizing whale teeth, the primary material of the art, was necessary by reason of their scarcity. If so, the old journals do not record many complaints about it, and with each adult whale yielding up to 50 teeth, the number of teeth taken on an average voyage could number in the thousands. That should have been enough for all in the average whale-ship crew of 28, even with a particularly close-fisted mate doing the dole.

There is another school of thought which holds the word scrimshaw to be from an archaic Dutch word meaning "lazy fellow," but that is disputed, as are the theories of one or two scholars who postulate an American Indian origin.

Others argue it is British and point to the word *scrimshank*, which, in the British military, was used synomously for the word *shirk* — avoiding duty. Norm Flayderman makes a case for a possible Chinese origin of the word, then ends his discussion of the matter with the thought that it might even be from somewhere in the South Seas.

Having noted in his journal of 1844 all the various scrimshaw'd artifacts which his shipmates had underway, Gurdon Hall records his own activity:

> *"Got up a couple of Sperm Teeth, scraped them off Smooth ready to polish. Have some idea of Scratching a little something on them to make them look as Curious as possible . . ."*

Somehow the glass of the case does not interfere so much with our examination of the crafted artifacts, the jagging wheels, swifts, canes and boxes, but the whale teeth with their engravings seem to be prisoners standing there in tidy ranks. Some have little mirrors behind them to allow the viewer to glimpse the side that doesn't show.

CORSET BUSKS were also popular scrimshaw projects, uncomplicated of shape, with flat surfaces. Made of wood, baleen or bone, they were 10 to 12 inches long, and were inserted in a vertical pocket in the front of a woman's corset to keep the garment from bunching when tightly laced. The busk at the left is bone, dated 1701, shows flowers, a casket with mourner, and the legend: "When Liveing respected, when dead lemented." The busk to the right, also bone, hopes a sweet heart will "Forget me not."

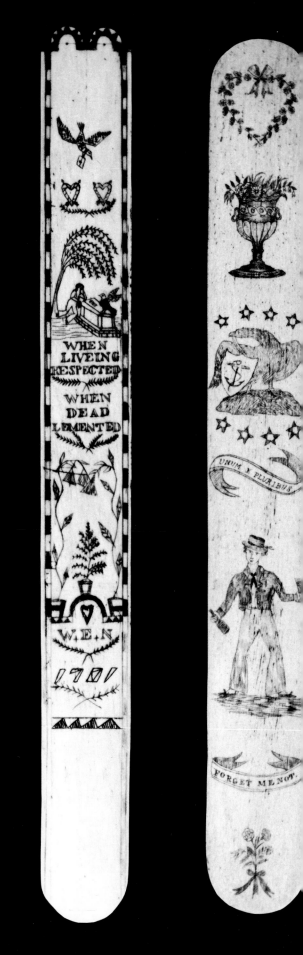

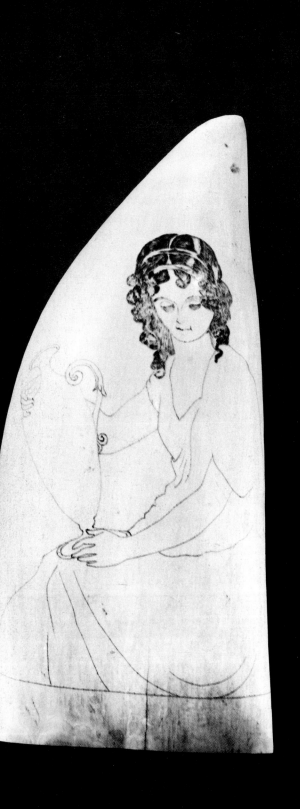

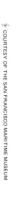

They are not flat graphic art and they are not sculpture. They are a combination of the two, each one a miniature, curving mural on an ivory free-form made by nature in a whale's mouth. Each asks to be held in the hand and turned and fondled as it is examined. That is a great part of the charm of the art form — to touch.

The subjects engraved on the teeth were limitless, although the means and tools were quite simple. The last chapter of this book is devoted to the actual process by which such ivory engraving is done. Of course ships were depicted again and again, and other nautical motifs; but lots of non-nautical scenes were, too. The sailing ship hands who etched scrimshaw were bound by no rules. There was no Academy to impose any. Being a folk art it was primitive, with no formal teachers, and no reward other than the doing of it. There was nothing to inhibit the artist's freedom of subject, imagination or style.

Understandably, women were a favorite subject, all kinds. There survive etchings of sailor's wives, Indian princesses, angels with harps, blindfold Justices with scales and swords, Liberties in stars and stripes, Highland Lassies in tartan, Lady Godivas in hair, wives of presidents, ladies of fashion, Brittania, hula dancers, shepherdesses, Greek goddesses, Nubians, sweethearts, lady pirates, daughters, queens, nymphs, actresses, madonnas, mermaids, amazons, and trollops.

A few of the human figures and portraits found on teeth and walrus tusks are skillfully done, but not very many. Added to the natural difficulty of graphically depicting the human form was a further trial for those untrained artists — the incompatability of their medium with the female form itself.

The human body is warm, soft, supple,

but the etched line is brittle and hard. The best of the scrimshaw'd figures were generally copied from magazines of the day. The piece on page 14 illustrates an exceptionally facile engraving by an unknown sailor who left the graceful lady unfinished for some reason. It is an unusual view of an old piece of work in progress.

As we examine the old scrimshaw in the museum case, we realize that the hand of the scrimshander moved with much less effort when it was depicting patriotic themes, ships or any of the many other subjects used: geometrical designs, public monuments, endless floral patterns, cannons going off, coats of arms, sunsets, maps, horse races, Home Sweet Home, political cartoons such as the cigar-chomping Uncle Sam menacing the Boxer rebel on this page, vases, pots, erupting volcanos, ascension balloons, buildings, banners and battles — especially sea battles, naturally (see page 6).

Teeth of all sizes were used, but generally the biggest teeth were the most highly prized, in some cases no doubt because of their value as trophies of a particularly big or formidable whale. Clifford Ashley wrote: "There never yet has been found (a whale tooth) large enough to turn out a full-sized billiard ball."

However, scrimshander and collector Rick Yager owns a whale tooth from which a standard ivory two and three-eighth-inch billiard ball could be cut with a full eighth-inch to spare all the way around. Also, the carving of a skull on page 82 was cut from a whale tooth which was not graceful enough to lend itself to engraving, but had enough meat of ivory from which to cut the billiard ball sized piece.

While exceptional, other teeth of this size are to be found in most of the large museum collections of scrimshaw, though

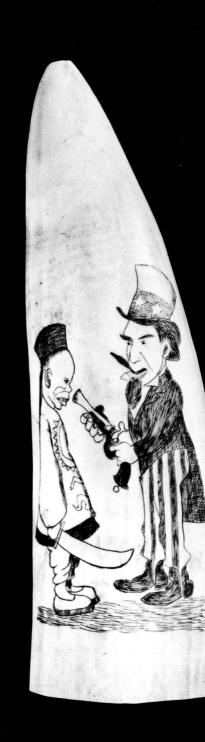

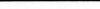

they are not always engraved or on display. The largest of the lot are probably those in a pair owned by the New Bedford Whaling Museum. They are unadorned and together weigh eight pounds, 11 ounces. The photographs of whale teeth appearing throughout this book usually show the pieces close to life size, excepting items such as above and on the next page, which are too large to reproduce full size.

So we see that scrimshaw can be divided into two main categories: A.) Engraving in ivory, sometimes bone (see pages 13 and 17), or in baleen, though less frequently. Most such engraving was done on whale teeth, which has become a distinct art form of its own.

B.) Crafted artifacts fashioned from the various woods, bones, metals, baleens, pearl shell, amber, all the ivories — whale, walrus, elephant, narwhal and, though rarely, even hippopotamus — tortoise shell, ostrich eggs, coconut shells and swordfish and sawfish blades, whatever a sailor could swap for or catch.

These materials were worked with the simplest hand tools, sometimes into the very fabric of the ship itself. Whalerman and author Herman Melville describes his *Pequod* as follows:

"She was a thing of trophies. A cannibal of a craft, tricking herself forth in the chased bones of her enemies. All 'round, her unpannelled, open bulwarks were garnished like one continuous jaw, with the long sharp teeth of the sperm whale, inserted there for pins, to fasten her old hempen thews and tendons to. Those ran not through base blocks of landwood, but deftly travelled over sheaves of sea-ivory. Scorning a turnstile wheel at her reverend helm, she sported there a tiller; and that tiller was in one mass, curiously carved from the long narrow jaw of her hereditary foe. The helmsman who steered by that tiller in a tempest felt like the Tarter, when he holds back his fiery steed by clutching its jaw. A noble craft, but somehow a most melancholy! All noble things are touched with that."

By 1880 the whaling capital of the world had shifted from the east coast of the United States to the west, where it was concentrated in San Francisco. The Civil War had severely crippled the great New England whaling fleet, which

PANBONE slab, here greatly reduced in size, shows two vessels amongst a pod of whales. The ship at the left is hove to, cutting in with two kills alongside. The bark at the right follows her boats, close hauled, as they pursue their prey.

16

sustained a further disaster in 1871 when 31 ships were lost in the polar ice.

Rock oil had been discovered and tapped and was challenging whale oil commercially. The fleet never recovered. Many of the remaining Yankee whalers sailed into the Pacific to stay, re-registering in San Francisco. Today's only surviving whaling vessel, the bark *Charles W. Morgan*, now a floating museum at Mystic Seaport, Connecticut, fished out of San Francisco for 20 years.

The whalermen brought their art with them to the west coast with the arrival of the first whale ships early in the century. It was in time adopted in various forms by the Eskimos, who had been working with walrus ivory for centuries. From the whalers they learned new engraving techniques, and they still carry on the art form.

The favorite Eskimo scrimshaw pieces, judging from the numbers done, are their cribbage boards (see page 16). These are made from walrus tusks, then engraved with game animals, hunting or fishing scenes, sometimes maps, sometimes carvings of dog teams and sleds, caribou, seals, or even the walrus himself, in miniature.

Scrimshaw caught on in many places. Prisoners of war in various European conflicts had long done scrimshaw-like work of many kinds, but during the American Revolution and the War of 1812, thousands of Yankee seamen, many of them ex-whalermen, brought their scrimshaw work to the prison ships of England, where they taught their craft to many, and in turn probably learned something from others, such as the ivory-carvers of Dieppe, their sometimes gaolmates.

Aboard a prison ship there wasn't the tumble of the open sea, and there was all the time in the world for elaboration, so great works were undertaken. Fully-rigged ships were built of soup bones sawn into thin slabs, then stripped into tiny planks the thickness of a playing card, the width of a match.

The vessel could thus be constructed from the keel up. She would be fastened, perhaps, with nails of bone smaller in diameter than pins, and each one of course carefully carved. For the most part glue was unavailable.

Of prison pieces other than ship models, it is sometimes difficult to tell the work done by sailors from that done by soldiers. Much was done, and much survives, especially from the two decades of Napoleonic wars, during which it was created by men from all the European nations, besides Great Britain and America.

Also scrimshawing away by the second half of the last century were seamen on merchant vessels and sailing men-of-war. Their production of the art was smaller

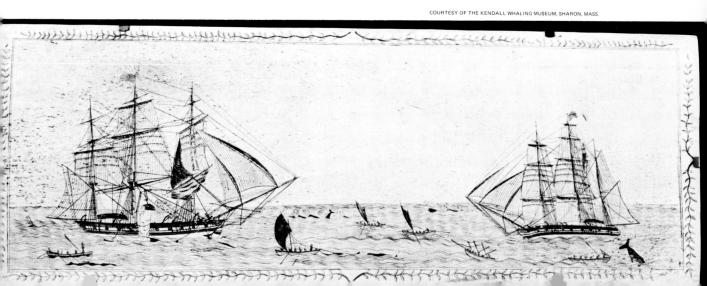

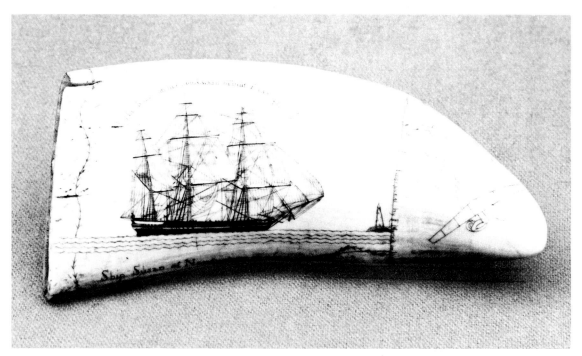

BEST KNOWN of the antique scrimshaw is by whalerman Frederick Myrick, seaman aboard ship Susan, *portrayed above with all sail set, under the legend: "The Susan on her homeward bound passage." Myrick was one of the few old scrimshanders who engraved his pieces with signature, dates, names of crewmen, salty legends and ship's locations.*

than that of the whalermen because they were permitted less time. Nor did they have the whaler's ready access to ivory and bone. Still, they obtained material and found time to leave us many examples of the craft, particularly portraits of the warships and merchantmen aboard which they sailed.

While a whalerman could look forward to much more leisure time at sea than anyone other than a fellow fisherman, his whole allotment of time was by no means usable for scrimshaw. There was still much work to be done, above and below, aboard the whale ship, as with any other wind

Whale vessels were more leniently run, for which reason, along with their notorious smell, they were generally looked down upon by their brethren in the other maritime services, who called them blubber buckets and other things less generous.

machine. If a sailor's free time fell at night, there was no adequate light. For etching of any quality that would also apply to early morning and evening as well, and also to cloudy days or foggy ones.

To see what one is doing at all in white-line-on-white-surface engraving, the artist needs a glare-spot on the work created by strong, direct light. On board a sailing vessel that will only be the bright sunlight on deck. Misty weather provides sufficient light for whittling or carving, but not for etching.

Further, though the light might permit, sea and weather conditions might not. A stiff breeze with blown spray and wet decks is not conducive to close engraving. Even mildly cold weather makes fingers too stiff for sensitive, fine work.

No doubt much of the crudeness so frequently found in old scrimshaw work is

18

because that work was done under less than ideal conditions.

One of the most frequently asked questions today about scrimshaw is, "What is it worth?" A monetary value is inevitably demanded. This is a subject generally avoided by scrimshaw historians and those who have written on the art. There is, of course, no general answer.

Pieces are individually evaluated. In general, scrimshaw demand (and therefore price) took a great leap during and after the presidency of the late John F. Kennedy. He was a scrimshaw enthusiast, and that fact greatly popularized the art form. Since his death, scrimshaw prices have doubled, trebled, quadrupled, and the attics and basements have yielded up forgotten treasures.

As with most things, the value of a piece of antique scrimshaw depends on the quality of the work, the condition of the piece and how much data about itself it offers. Authentic, signed, dated pieces are rare, therefore in demand.

Makers of old scrimshaw were not all that frequently given to dating their work, although a few did. For the most part the date meant nothing to them except another day of endless ocean. Nor did they sign their work, and their consequent anonymity makes the work of any one who *is* known very valuable.

Considered today the most famous scrimshander of the last century, Frederick Myrick was a crewman between 1826 and 1830 on the whale ship *Susan.* For this reason, the nine or so surviving examples of his work from those years are known as The Susan's Teeth, and they are probably the most dollar-valuable scrimshaw around. One of Myrick's pieces sold at auction recently for $11,000, probably the highest price paid to date for any piece of scrimshaw.

Why so much?

The *Susan's* voyage is well-documented in existing manuscripts. The teeth Myrick engraved aboard her have been cited again and again over the years as examples of the art, and have been prized items in very large collections and unavailable for sale.

The example appearing on page 23 is representative. It is signed and dated as well as engraved with a salty legend:

"Death to the Living, Long Life to the Killers"

Another favorite Myrick legend:

"Success to Sailor's Wives, Greasy Luck to Whalers"

The teeth have a sameness to them. Myrick was apparently not ambitious to create more imaginative work, and having found a happy design he stuck with it. Usually this included a profile view of the ship, the name of her skipper, her position, an anchor, crossed flags.

He was a more talented engraver than most, as far as technical facility is concerned, and his work is spacious, dignified and clean. It is just about the only old scrimshaw around which can be identified by label, like a painting: "We have a Rembrandt." In this case, "We have a Susan's Tooth."

As this book is being written, so much is changing that it seems silly to devote much time to a discussion of values. By tomorrow they will have changed. Recent legislation has placed heavy restrictions on the free circulation of sperm whale teeth, new or old, and nobody knows what the outcome will be.

The law has been challenged, and an amendment is at this moment before the

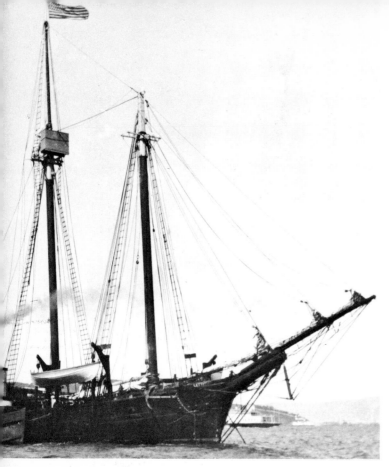

LETTITIA: *"Most of her crew were in their bunks."*

U.S. legislature which will, if passed, again allow free trade in scrimshaw. This is discussed more fully in Chapter III.

Back to our museum for at least a moment before leaving it. We have traced the history of whaling from continent to continent, through its rise as an industry and into its decline.

One by one the old ships vanished. Some were crushed in polar ice, some disappeared, swallowed up by the sea, others were allowed to become more and more decrepit until they disintegrated, worked to death by ship owners who did not include repair and overhaul in their budgets.

Here is an incident from the twilight days of whaling as recorded by Karl Kortum writing down the words of Jack Shickell, a boat puller aboard the whaler *Lettitia.* This vessel met with the bark *Gay Head* (see pages 21, 31 and 43) in 1912 for a gam, the traditional exchange of visits between crew and officers of whaling ships meeting at sea. *Lettitia* was a 245-ton schooner (see pages 20, 31 and 42) fishing out of San Francisco, making her last whaling cruise under "Sperm Whale Jimmy" Macomber:

"I'll never forget what a pretty sight she made, the *Gay Head,* as she closed with us and rounded to for a gam. The *Lettitia* was a big, heavy schooner and I don't think *Gay Head* was many tons larger, but being a bark she handled smartly.

"You should have seen her come about; she spun right on her heel. She was handled just like a sloop out here in the Bay. Of course, they were ballasted right. They would shift around the barrels of whale oil as need be. Like ourselves, she didn't have much of a catch.

"That was June 13, 1912. It had been pre-arranged. The rendezvous was to be in the vicinity of Cape St. Elias, but offshore. There would be no chance that way for any of us to take a boat and head for the beach. One week before the gam Mt. St. Elias, a volcano, erupted. For a few days we had been subjected to a dust storm of pumice.

"As you can imagine, the arrival of the *Gay Head* caused quite a stir aboard *Lettitia.* Most of the crew were in their bunks, as usual, when she hove in sight, but soon all hands were on deck to watch the little bark come about and round to under our stern. I was the only man forward who had put in time in square sail and it was a sight I shall always remember. When the order came to lower mate's boat, I was ready. I pulled number one oar, it being a short one and me a light yard man.

"In the meantime, *Gay Head,* too, had

dropped a boat, and her skipper was already on the way across to gam with Captain Macomber. I had hopes of being able to go aboard the bark, but this was denied us as it turned out.

"Nobody but Mr. Hiller, the mate (and later master) of *Lettitia* went on board to gam. So we sat in the pitching boat and swapped insults with the forward crew of the *Gay Head.* We had brought a few parcels and a little sack of mail for her, but that was handled by her captain.

"The gam lasted less than half an hour. A whale had been sighted earlier that day, but lost track of, and our Old Man was anxious to get going in search of him again. The two vessels parted, each going its own way.

"Shortly after this, Captain Macomber died of a heart attack after the excitement of finding that we were in the middle of a big pod of sperm whales. He had gone aloft to keep track of the two boats out, and then down to the deck to stir up the men working onboard, who were cutting into one we had alongside. The mate brought the *Lettitia* back to San Francisco.

"In 1912 there were three of us whale fishing (in the Pacific), the *John and Winthrop,* the *Gay Head* and *Lettitia.* We never saw the *John and Winthrop.*

"At the time it happened, we did not fully appreciate the significance of the two whaling vessels rendezvousing. It proved to be the last gam held in the North Pacific, or any other ocean, I suppose. *Gay Head* went north again in 1913. Had I known of it, I might have that voyage too, but by that time I was halfway around the world again in the barkentine *Aurora.*

"1913 was the year the Old Man came back disgusted. The grounds were just about fished out. He had a good westerly to take him up Oakland Creek, so he blew for the drawbridge, which just got opened

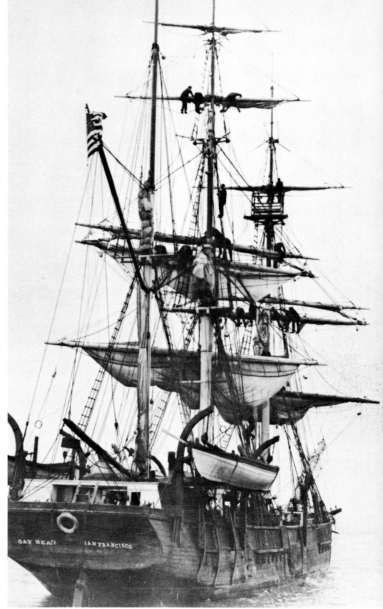

GAY HEAD: *"She handled smartly . . . like a sloop."*

up in time, and sailed her right on up onto the mudflats. He would have rammed her right through that bridge if they hadn't opened it.

"*Gay Head* went north one more year, 1914, and was wrecked at Chignik, Alaska. *Lettitia,* I'm told, capsized in a blow while she lay at anchor on the mudflats off South City a few years later."

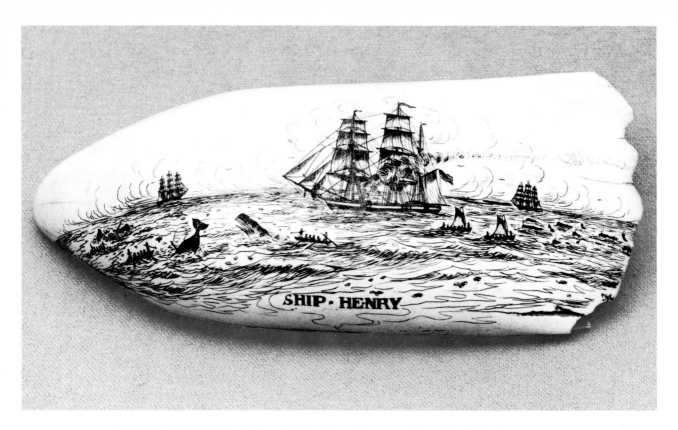

WILLIAM PERRY of New Bedford was born at the end of the last century into a whaling family and learned whaling lore young, although he never sailed in a working square rigger. Nonetheless, he engraved teeth prodigiously and became the first of the new scrimshanders.

II Scrimshaw: The New

The new scrimshaw of today is the old scrimshaw of tomorrow. Where then is the dividing line between *old* and *new* from our present vantage point? Let's paste our own *old* label on everything done before 1924. In that year the last square-rigged Yankee whaling vessel, the bark *Wanderer*, sailed from New Bedford on a voyage after oil. Less than 24 hours out, she was struck by a hurricane which blew her onto the rocks of Buzzards Bay. And that was more or less the end of that. However, the parent was survived by the child.

Scrimshaw, the art the whalers began, continued. There remained (and still remain) people for whom the plain surface of a tooth or tusk triggers something in the imagination whereby designs begin to form ghostlike on the ivory, where no designs actually exist. Twitching to materialize them there, the hand reaches for something with which to scratch. It is the burden of the scrimshander.

One such was William Perry of New Bedford. He has been called the last of the old scrimshanders. Under our labeling system he is the first of the new, although much of his

22

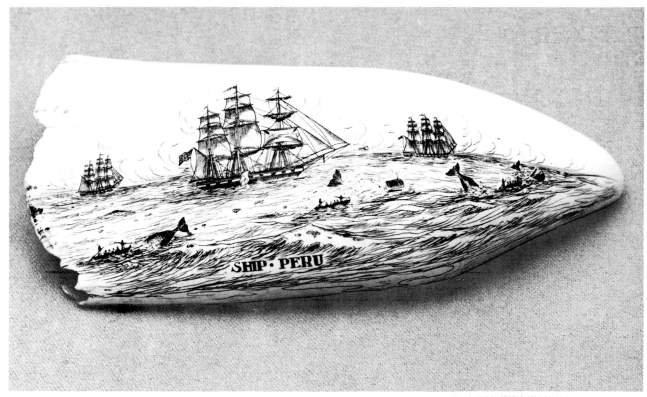

TWO TEETH on these pages portray examples of Perry's work. His career, in total, spanned the entire period of scrimshaw's eclipse, between the time of the last of the old Yankee whale ships and the public's re-discovery of the whalerman's folk art some four decades later.

scrimshaw is prominently displayed in several large collections, including those at the New Bedford and the Nantucket whaling museums.

His career as a scrimshander seems to have been getting under way just about the time *Wanderer* went ashore. He was then 29. He was from New Bedford, and wanted to go whaling when he was a teenager, but his mother would not let him, so he followed various other careers. These included a job as second cook on a lightship and a seven-year stint as a caretaker aboard the *Charles W. Morgan*. All his life he scrimshaw'd prolifically, engraving around 1000 teeth, according to his own estimate, before his death a few years ago. Most of them depicted whaling scenes, such as those engraved on the piece depicted front and reverse above.

Some of his work he gave away to friends, but he supplemented his income with his art, most of which he sold through marine curio shops. Besides scrimshawing whale teeth, he engraved silver and aluminum medals, fixed jewelry, and painted whaling ships in oil. Perry never in his life voyaged on a working sailing vessel, but produced scrimshaw into the

23

1960's. Other scrimshanders were at work in the 30's, 40's and 50's, but Perry was the most prolific and best known. His scrimshaw career spanned the whole period between the end of the whaling era and the time when America re-awakened to the existence of an art form which was peculiarly her own, an awakening much inspired by President Kennedy.

YANKEE whale ship skipper studies charts in a scene out of Ashley, scrimshaw'd by Milton Delano, one of the best known of today's scrimshaw artists.

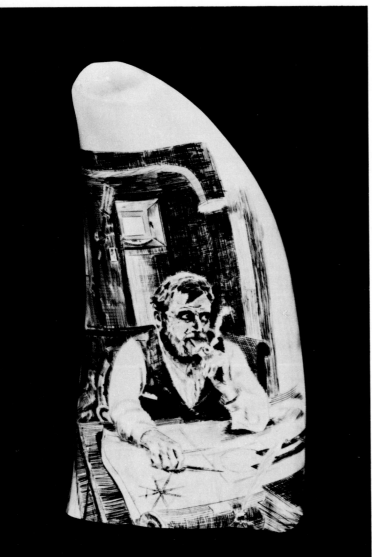

Although the Kennedy scrimshaw collection is small and contains no individual pieces of any tremendous significance, its historical impact on the art as a whole is quite considerable, for Kennedy's collection surrounded him in his White House office and was much photographed and publicized.

Of the 34 engraved whale teeth and three walrus tusks owned by President Kennedy, a number were quite new work, including one commissioned by Jacqueline Kennedy from scrimshander Milton Delano depicting the Presidential Seal.

It was given to the President as a gift, and was later placed in his casket by Mrs. Kennedy and interred with his remains, making it unquestionably the most valuable but inaccessible piece of contemporary scrimshaw. It has been illustrated in a number of books and articles about the art. Another example of Delano's work appears on this page.

The abrupt awareness of scrimshaw as a part of the national heritage of the United States created an immediate impact on the art. All the antique work was sucked from the shelves of the shops and galleries that had any for sale, driving prices up and creating an instant demand for more of the work.

This inevitably inspired two additional breeds of scrimshaw makers, and their work bears discussion for, although they did not surface until the early 1960's, they have been prolific. These are the forgers of old scrimshaw and the mass-producers of new. Between them they have created by far the bulk of the work done in the last dozen years.

Mass-produced scrimshaw has deluged the gift counters of the American coasts for the past decade with cuff links, tie tacks, desk sets, etc. Although most collectors have no interest in this work, it has

"Dear Scrimshaw Pal..."

The etched tooth pictured on page 27 is by Rick Yager, a long time collector of scrimshaw as well as a scrimshander himself. To the public he is best known as the man who drew the late comic strip *Buck Rogers in the 25th Century*. Last year Mr. Yager formally swore off doing any more scrimshaw, in rage and frustration over the high price of a batch of whale teeth offered for sale by the widow of a deceased sea captain. As he put it in a letter to the author, "I am through, repeat, through with scrimshaw. I feel like a butterfly collector in Northern Siberia in winter, with lots of enthusiasm, but no materials. At least, none I can afford unless I knock over a bank." The author immediately sent Mr. Yager a medium sized tooth to tide him over. Yager's response to the gift is printed here as a document which is more than usually revelatory about the state of a scrimshander's art and mind, his trials, his joys and some areas in between:

Dear Scrimshaw Pal:

Getting the whale tooth gift in the mail was, needless to say, a high point in my dull existence. Have you ever noticed the truly beautiful sound the thumping of a whale tooth makes as it moves back and forth in an unopened package? To me it is the loveliest sound of all. In fact, I did not open the box until the next day because once the box is opened, the magic is gone.

Putting the tooth back and resealing the box just does not work out; there is a falseness about it. Some day when I'm rich I'd like to hire a great symphony orchestra to play something like the William Tell Overture, *only instead of their regular instruments, they'd each have a whale tooth in an unopened box with about an inch clearance at each end, so they could be thumped musically to and fro.*

It is true I was going to give the whole scrimshaw thing up before your tooth arrived. I got a letter from the Widow and she wanted $450.00 for twelve whale's teeth that aren't too big. I think the old gal must be a little flakey. Her prices are a cinch for Onassis or Hughes.

I sure wish when the getting was good I'd layed in a supply, for there was a woman dealer in Europe who sent me huge polished teeth for $3.00 each and used to apologize for the high price she had to charge. That was back about 1961. I also knew a guy in Massachusetts who had thousands of 'em. Nine-inchers were seven bucks.

Anyway, the big and important thing right now is to get those other teeth you talked about. When I told you my scrimshaw days were over, it was the lack of teeth that forced me to it. So when you mentioned the possibility of some other teeth which we could get without having to deal with the widow, I fairly flipped. Would I like some? I'll say. Let's get 'em all if we can. How big are they?

The biggest whale tooth I ever got cost $4.50 and came from a place where you can no longer get them. However, they do have Sperm Whale ear bones, a fairly big supply, if you're interested in them. They are good

25

to scrimshaw, big, heavy and strangely shaped. A lady writer about the ocean once noted that if it ever dried up, the most noticeable things left on the bottom would be vast numbers of shark teeth and Sperm Whale earbones, both of which are nearly indestructible.

Anyway, last time I was at that place with the earbones, I was with a couple of pals, and they each got one or two Sperm Whale eyeballs embedded in clear plastic. They are huge (about the size of a bowling ball) and wierd looking, and I didn't get one because I didn't want the thing staring at me around the house.

Now, friend William, I cannot any longer hold back the comment my conscience bids me make to you. I hope you will abandon the fantasy themes you sometimes put in your scrimshaw. I hope you will abandon them altogether and just be a scrimshaw purist. There is no place for any fantasy on whale teeth, particularly now that they are so scarce. It dismays me somewhat, for the subjects in whaling are endless and wonderful. I, myself, know all about fantasy, having drawn a fantasy — adventure strip for 26 years. But the subjects for scrimshawing in the old tradition are far too numerous to necessitate seeking elsewhere for subjects.

Ships in storms, in calms, whale barks caught in the polar ice, rounding the horn in a gale, trying out the oil, attacking the whale, attacked by the whale, the girl back home, shields with eagles, anchors, the American flag . . . I've made eagles in so many poses you couldn't count 'em. Sperm whales, too, and all the rest. The possibilities are endless! Therefore when I read a year or so ago about a guy somewhere scrimshawing Rocky Mountain Big Horns and Winnie-the-Pooh on whale teeth it made me want to throw up.

There. I've said my say. Needless to mention, I've secretly hated that Winnie-the-Pooh guy for demeaning the great and honorable fraternity of real, honest-to-gosh New Bedford, Nantucket, Sag Harbor scrimshanders of the Present Day.

Last night I had a dream, by the way, inspired perhaps by my thoughts of the Widow's teeth. A big box arrived, and I hurriedly opened it. It was full of whale teeth that were unbelievable! The first one I withdrew from the box was a giant tooth, about 15 inches long, the most fantastic scrimshaw I've ever seen. Just picture the most exquisite steel engraving. That's how it was. Too perfect to describe. It pictured a polar bear standing on an ice floe staring out at the viewer, like Uncle Sam in the famous war poster, and when you looked straight at it the bear's eyes were lighted up with a bright amber glow, while the whole tooth shimmered with an unearthly transluscence.

And each one got better! I unwrapped tooth after tooth, and then, as I was opening what I knew was to be the largest, most sensational tooth of all, I woke up. Darn it!

Just thinking about those wonderful whale teeth makes me get all numb and lose speech co-ordination, so I'm going to start ending this letter now.

If it were to come to pass that I got some of those other whale teeth you mentioned, then I would race to my scrimshaw workbox, great tears of uncontrolled joy streaming from my eyes, and prepare once again to bring forth on the beautiful ivory surface — not Winnie the Pooh, not a mountain goat, not a farm scene from the Russian Steppe, not a diesel locomotive, but a beautiful whaling bark ploughing the waves of a distant sea, with perhaps an eagle and shield on the other side surrounded by stars, banners and the girl back home.

Best regards, etc.

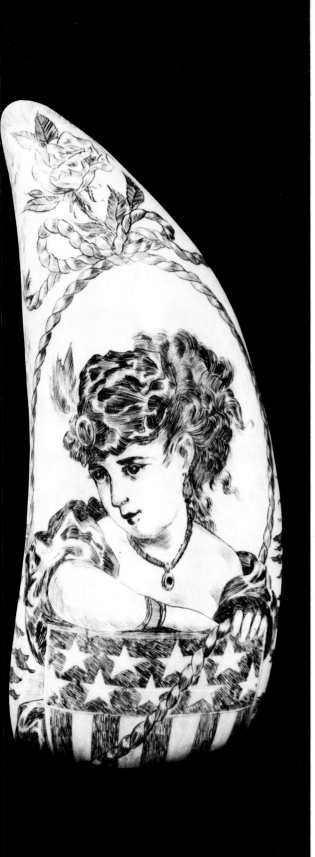

served a purpose, having made some small piece of ivory etched with a nautical design available to every person who would own an example of scrimshaw.

True, much of it is repetitive in design, marketed to retailers by means of catalogue, each ship, anchor or lighthouse design with a code number for ease of ordering in quantity. President Kennedy's collection contains a couple of small teeth of this description.

But it is still hand work, or has been in the United States. An exception was a Japanese merchant who for a while produced scrimshaw by machine and marketed it in America. He used a device with 10 or so spring-loaded stylii on a follower-rod which duplicated the movements of a master-stylus manipulated by an engraver. Similarly shaped and sized teeth were locked into position, then quickly given identical designs by this process, which is probably industrial technology's closest approach to the art of scrimshaw. The results left much to be desired.

This and the less blatant methods of mass-producing scrimshaw on whale ivory were all doomed by laws which in 1973 entirely banned the importation of products made from the bodies of creatures which are listed as endangered species. Sperm whale teeth are included. This and subsequent legisiation (see Chapter III)

BUCK ROGERS creator Rick Yager, who did the tooth opposite, once happened upon a book about Yankee whaling: "By the time I had finished," he explains, "the briny smell of the ocean, the pungent odor of spermaceti oil, the choking reek of the try-pots, the sweaty stink of the fo'csle, the ice air of the Bering Sea had combined to make a scrimshaw addict."

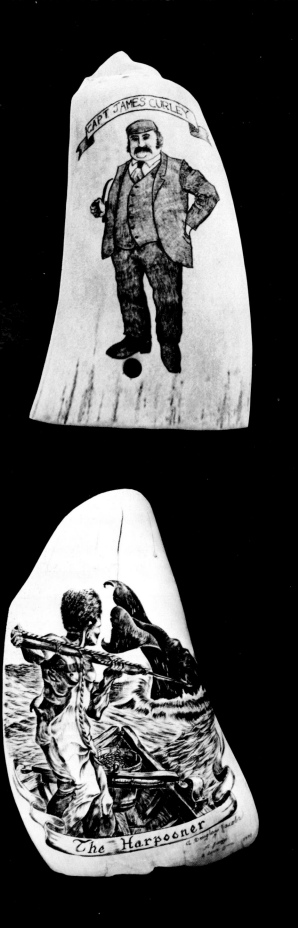

have entirely cut off any scrimshaw produced abroad, as well as the raw materials which fed the work being produced within the United States.

Forged scrimshaw is new work which imitates antique work and is misrepresented. It's hard to say how much of this is being done. For sheer volume it does not begin to approach the souvenir scrimshaw, but its makers are active, and some of them are very talented.

One director of a major New England Maritime Museum stopped purchasing any more scrimshaw for his institution.

"I got burned so many times, I finally decided to quit buying the stuff," he confessed. Another scrimshaw authority expresses doubt as to the authenticity of all the famous Susan's Teeth.

Meticulous forgers are unquestionably at work, possibly more so in scrimshaw than even the fields of old furniture, weapons, art, etc. Scrimshaw particularly invites forgery because the original work in general was anonymous, of mediocre artistry, and rather crudely wrought. Duplicating such antiques as furniture, paintings, postage stamps, and weaponry however, requires considerable resources, material, technical skill and knowledge.

There are a few general rules for identifying new work dressed as old. Many

TUGBOAT skipper Capt. James Curley is jauntily portrayed on a small tooth engraved by scrimshander William Horgos of San Francisco. Top left.

HARPOONER TENSES, whale dives in this somber, heavily engraved piece, below left, by A. Douglas Jacobs of Long Island, after a drawing in the Kendall Museum.

fakes are not very challenging. But no rules are effective against really skilled forgery, as the museum director learned.

Old ivory is frequently cracked, and whale teeth usually acquire a rich, orange-yellow patina, but not invariably. There are lots of exceptions that are known to be authentic.

Sometimes old ivory takes on a frosted appearance, or even a grey or a bluish hue, like the complexion of a very old person. Whale ivory when freshly polished has a creamy look which it loses within a very few years. And although splitting or cracking is frequently encountered in old ivory, new ivory may do the same, especially if subjected to heat.

As for that old, yellow look, there are many, many different stains and dyes which drive beneath the surface of ivory and become quite colorfast. Some are very convincing. Others don't look very real at all, such as evenly applied tea, although it is a popular dye much used by people who, while perhaps not forging teeth, want to color their work in passing to give it an antique-looking patina.

If a piece of allegedly old scrimshaw has a ship engraved on it, an examination of hull and rigging detail will very frequently turn up some telling error. Sailors seldom made technical mistakes pertaining to ships' gear, though their depictions were frequently crude. The gear was as familiar to them as their own shoelaces. But for today's artist who is not so intimately familiar with the intricacies and variations of hull and rig, there are very many traps.

There do not seem to be any really definitive methods for spotting clever bogus scrimshaw. Recently, a couple of years after scrimshaw collector-dealer-author Norman Flayderman published his massive *Scrimshaw and Scrimshanders*, he was questioned as to what positive identification

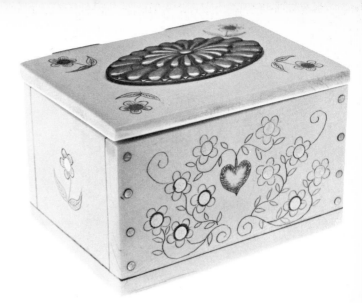

PHOTO BY STEPHEN FRISCH, SAUSALITO, CA

IVORY BOX, above, is by Marianne Fletcher of Mill Valley, California. It is engraved, inlaid with silver and pearl shell, pegged with brass pins.

CLIPPER SHIP LIGHTNING *is meticulously portrayed by the late Capt. Lloyd Anderson, U.S. Coast Guard, on a plaque of elephant ivory. Capt. Anderson at first made ship models on long sea voyages, then obtained whale teeth and took up scrimshaw. His work is displayed in the Oakland Museum, Oakland, California.*

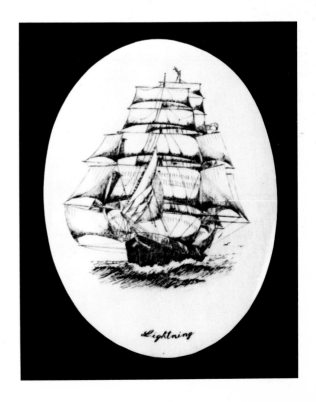

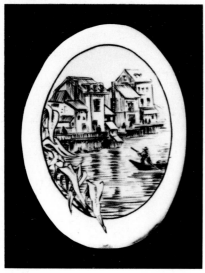

*OVAL PLAQUE is
by Steve Wilson, shows a
seaside scene: engraved
on a slab of ivory sliced
from a whale tooth.*

between new and old was possible (after the elementary techniques had been applied) when it came to a piece of scrimshaw that looked old but smelled bad.

Flayderman replied: "This of course is one of the keys to buying antique scrimshaw today, and it is very difficult to put into words an exacting method to do this. Of your statement: '. . . Looks good but smells bad,' I would say the very first and most basic premise to go on is exactly that. If it does smell bad in any way, then accept it as bad and leave it alone.

"This really holds true in just about all of the antique fields, and very much so in the antique scrimshaw field. It may be a 'seat of the pants' reasoning, but as one who lays his money on the line daily in buying and selling collector's items, and having observed the collecting field professionally, if it 'smells bad' it invariably is. Don't try to rationalize it from being bad into good. It rarely, if ever is. At least in my own experience, I have never found it to be. First impressions are very important."

One comment by Mr. Flayderman can especially be underlined. He speaks as a man who ". . . lays his money on the line . . .". Most authorities in collector's objects have become authorities not so much through books, although they are certainly aware of what's in the books, but by having dealt extensively with those objects for a long time; by handling many of them, gambling on their decisions, and having been fooled expensively a time or two. Hard as this is, it seems the best road to expertise.

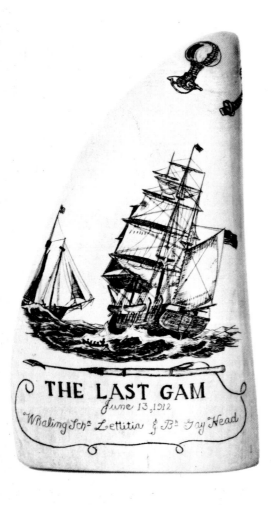

*LAST GAM tooth by C. R. Hull of Honolulu
commemorates the meeting between whalers*
Lettitia *and* Gay Head *described in first
chapter, and illustrated by photographs
on pages 20 and 21.*

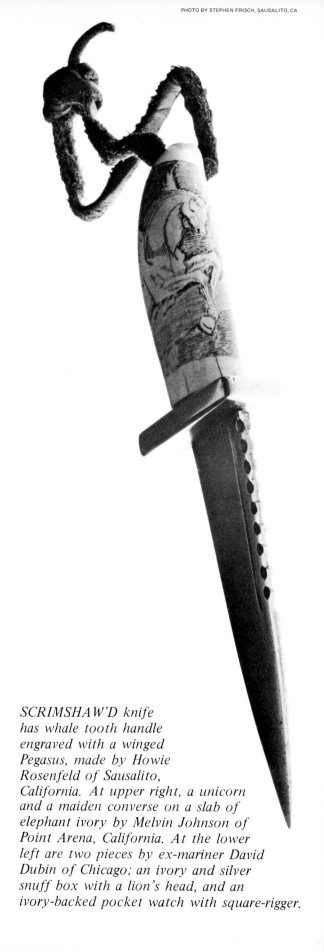

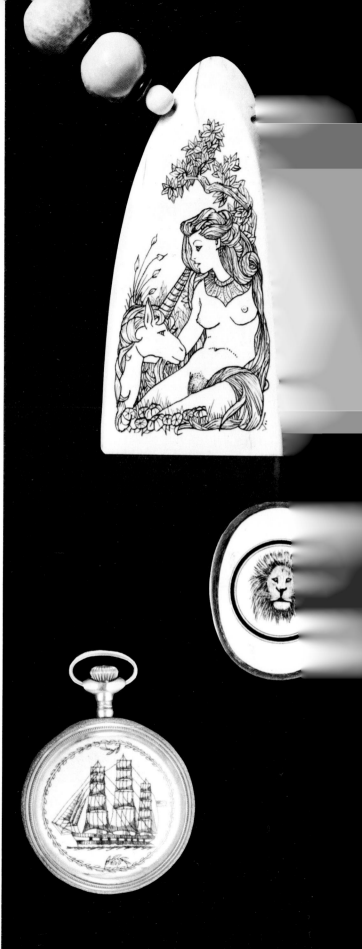

SCRIMSHAW'D knife has whale tooth handle engraved with a winged Pegasus, made by Howie Rosenfeld of Sausalito, California. At upper right, a unicorn and a maiden converse on a slab of elephant ivory by Melvin Johnson of Point Arena, California. At the lower left are two pieces by ex-mariner David Dubin of Chicago; an ivory and silver snuff box with a lion's head, and an ivory-backed pocket watch with square-rigger.

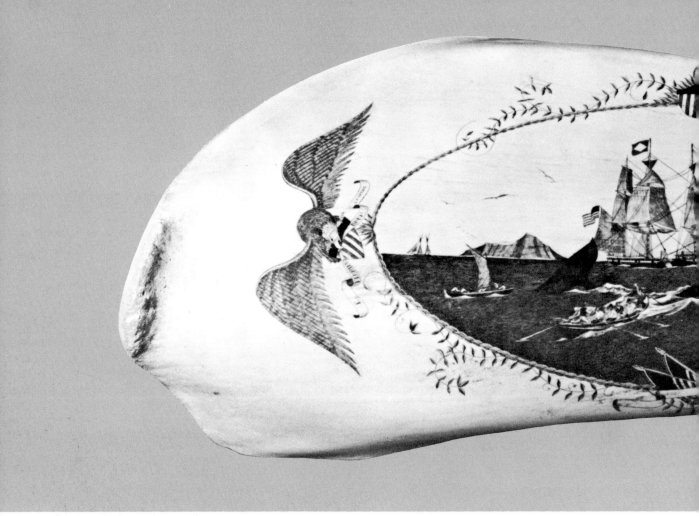

Some new scrimshaw is still being made by a few artists here and there who do it for the love of it. Some of these sell their work, and when they do, it is usually the best to be had. Some do it only as a hobby and sell none.

As a purely nautical art, scrimshaw has inevitably undergone dilution, but some of the scrimshanders are still maritime people, a few of them even working sailors under sail — yacht deliverers, charter skippers, crewmen, etc.

Rare as working sailing craft are, there remain a few, though the nature of their work has changed, and they are probably outnumbered by scrimshanders. In recent years various scrimshaw kits have even ap-peared, at first containing real whale teeth, lately plastic ones.

Old ships are more than ever the favor-ite theme of the scrimshander. There's something wistful about this tendency to depict the days of sail on thousands of tie-bars, cuff-links and teeth. The scrim-shanders who actually worked those old wind machines many times found the real-ity of their life under sail to be less than inspirational, and took their scrimshaw themes from their imagination, which was often far from the sea. There is sometimes this separation between the professional and the romantic.

For example, I was once asked by mas-ter boat builder Dean Stephens to decorate

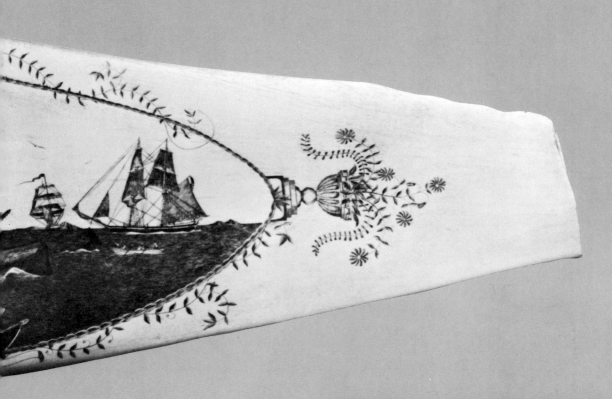

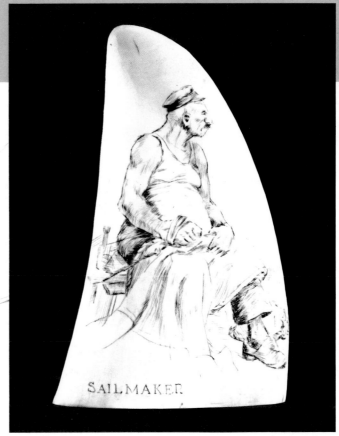

PAN BONE, the entire rear part of a sperm whale's jaw, above, is greatly reduced in this reproduction showing the clean, sharply detailed work of Nantucket scrimshander Robert Spring, whose style is intricate and suggests bygone days, although it is among the best of the new.

UNDERSHIRTED sailmaker, at right, by Lyle Galloway of San Francisco, is a piece immediately recognizable as new work, contrasts with the style above. On this tooth, there is no desire by the artist to re-create a feeling of yesterday.

SAILMAKER

a salon bulkhead in the ketch *Charity,* the vessel which was his home.

The bargain was made. Stephens would do some needed carpentry on my *Griffyn* (pages 70, 71) in return for a small mural in his vessel. When the time came for the work to begin, he was questioned as to what sort of sailing ship he wanted in the painting.

"None," he replied without hesitation. "No boats."

Not a ship? Well, what then? He considered for a moment, his eyes misting slightly.

"Cows," he said at last.

Cows?

"Yep. Cows. Chewing on some grass, with maybe a red barn and ploughed fields on a sunny day with no wind. It's gotta be a calm day. Maybe some horses too."

But, why?

"Listen," said Stephens, "When I'm out there somewhere, all reefed down, and every other wave coming right on over us, with everything wet and cold like that, do you think I want to come down off watch

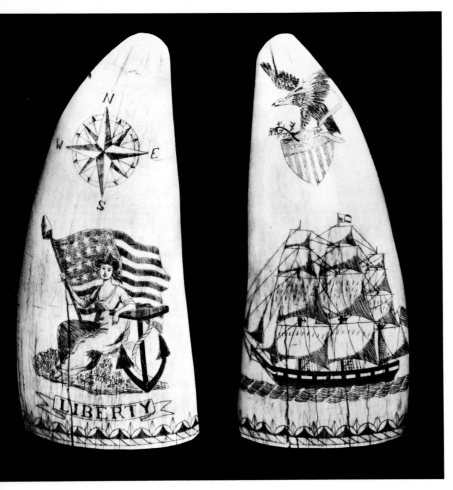

ANCIENT appearing whale tooth, right, shows front and back views, complete with cracks, old patina, old style. It is no forgery, but could be if the artist misrepresented his work. He does not. Federal Judge Paul E. Vardeman, its scrimshander, enjoys simulating the old. Vardeman lives in Missouri.

BELT BUCKLE, upper right, is by Eric Fletcher of Mill Valley, California; made of silver and elephant ivory. The plaque is engraved with a gaff cutter and schooner.

34

and have to look at another boat? No sir. I want to look at cows. Cows and green grass."

(For the contrasting view, that of the romanticist, the reader is referred to the letter by Rick Yager on page 25.)

Generally speaking, the scrimshander of today seems to copy more than his forbears. Possibly this is because there's more material to copy from today, and access to it. There is that tendency to think of the art form as an old one, the desire to make new work look old, even when there's no thought of actual misrepresentation.

Not to say the old sailors and whalers did not copy; on the contrary, many copied freely from periodicals and magazines of their day, but they had no forbears to imitate. They did their own work and it was work of their own age. They were unhandicapped by historical precedent.

In the case of scrimshanders of our own time who do create their own designs and ideas, the work tends to show considerably more sophistication and probably a generally higher level of skill, though frequently not the painstaking devotion to an individual piece that was lavished by the scrimshander of yesterday.

The scrimshaw artist of our own time has many obvious advantages his forbears did not. He has probably had some kind of art lessons and the leisure of the push-button society in which to pursue them. He has the aid of good artificial illumination, various sophisticated magnifying devices, commercial inks and fixatives, power tools for cutting and polishing ivory, and packages of sandpaper in convenient gradations of grit. Any old salt with his piece of sharkskin would have given much for some of these wonders, although others he might have considered more dubiously.

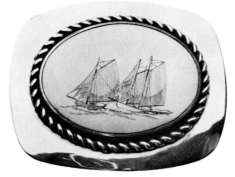

PHOTO BY STEPHEN FRISCH, SAUSALITO, CA

He would have coveted today's inexpensive paperbound books full of reproductions by Schöngauer, Mantegna, Dürer, Rembrandt, Brueghel and such. These long dead masters still hold the answers. The only art lesson the whalerman could muster was the occasional battered copy of *Godey's Ladies's Book,* or possibly the cover of a *Harper's Weekly.*

One kind of scrimshaw does seem to be dying out. No longer are the crafted implements being created, and all the rolling pins, walking sticks, jagging wheels and other such artifacts are things of the past. The amateur scrimshander doesn't seem to want to take the time in our accelerated age for work which is so demanding of time.

Even a fairly plain carved walking stick takes as much time to make as two or three engraved teeth. The very ornate stick on page 74 absorbed some 150 hours in a well-equipped shop. Nor have the professional scrimshanders been doing crafted artifacts (always with the possible exception of forgers) for the same reason — because they take too much time, and there's no particular market for new jagging wheels or such like.

The big demand is for engraved whale teeth, and as this demand has increased, the availability of the raw material has decreased so rapidly it is now questionable how long the art form can continue to exist.

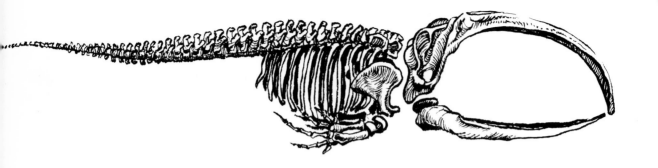

III An Endangered Species...

A half century after the last of the working Yankee whale barks perished on the rocks of Buzzards Bay, the last living legacy of the old whalermen, this peculiarly American folk art called scrimshaw, is at once threatened with extinction itself and at the same time at a peak of popularity. If it passes, we will of course always have the corpse of the art carefully preserved, the neat rows of yellowed teeth behind glass, untouchable to all except those who wipe the dust away.

The danger is to scrimshaw as a living art, just as the sperm whales are endangered as a living species, so that our only remembrance of them in future times might yet be a stuffed specimen or two hanging by wires from the ceiling of a natural history museum. Can both the whale and the art survive?

During the year in which this is being written, it is estimated over 37,500 whales will be killed. In the same period of time the whale bark *Wanderer* might have taken, say, a dozen. Maybe more. Perhaps less. Modern whaling techniques have been too efficient, too ruthless. No more do men risk their lives against a foe which might destroy them with one smack of the flukes; today we fire an explosive bomb from a safe distance into the body of a creature that has been stalked by helicopter and sonar.

Instinctively, many of us rebel at this slaughter. Perhaps we begin to smell our own destiny as a race of men somehow entwined with that of the whale, our ancient cousin and adversary. Or perhaps it all seems too impersonal, too unbalanced a match. Indeed, it is no match at all. Those times are long gone.

Between 1800 and 1928 we are told 487 whaling ships were lost at sea. Three of these are documented as having been rammed and sunk by enraged bull sperm whales. Some 33 captains were killed by the flukes or jaws of whales, as were 71 mates and 242 men, of which 36 were seen dragged into the depths, entangled in the lines of their own harpoons. These statistics were produced by methods that, though melancholy (as "all noble things are . . ."), are yet acceptable.

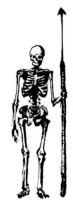

...An Endangered Art Form

It was not acceptable to Americans that by 1972 we were converting whales into cat food, cosmetics, and car wax. The last remnant of the American whale fishery was legislated out of existence, and a moratorium clamped on whaling. Other whaling nations have done likewise, though the giants of the industry have not. In the United States, legislation has followed legislation for the protection not only of the big cetaceans but many other endangered creatures as well.

Of all the legal verbiage contained in the new laws, that which most affects the scrimshaw art is found in Section 9, Paragraph E of *The Endangered Species Act of 1973,* which makes it against the law to "... deliver, receive, carry, transport or ship in interstate or foreign commerce, by any means whatsoever and in the course of a commercial activity ..." or to kill or to import any body parts of the creatures listed as endangered species. It makes few exceptions. The penalties are fines, prison sentences or both, and so it may fairly be said it is a law with teeth in it.

On top of the federal restrictions, which still allow intrastate commerce, a number of individual states have adopted laws of their own prohibiting commercial activity in such material.

What effect has all this legislation had on whaling?

Very little. Carrying on vigorously are the Japanese and the Russians who together were taking some 84 per-cent of the whales when the United States and the other countries honoring the current moratorium discontinued their activities. Roughly seven per-cent of all the meat consumed in Japan is whale.

That nation does not yet seem inclined to abandon whaling, despite real pressure at this time from America to do so. The wholesale destruction continues of mammals thought to be possibly as intelligent as man, although of an order of intelligence we do not understand.

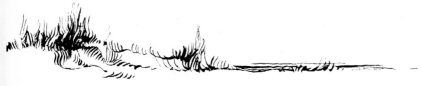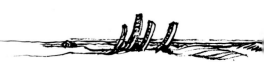

What effect have the laws had on scrimshaw?

Quite a lot. While the Japanese have literally millions of whale teeth to grind up for fertilizer, there is the beginning of a whale tooth black market in the United States, and there have been arrests and convictions for their smuggling. A spare tire loaded, not with hashish or pot, but whale teeth? Strange but true in our strange times.

Many scrimshanders (including this one) have turned to other kinds of ivory to engrave, primarily that of the elephant and walrus, creatures which are not *yet* listed as candidates for extinction, or other material entirely — paper or canvas. Some artists continue to work on whale teeth from reserves of the material gathered in the decade before the moratorium, when literally hundreds of tons of whale ivory came in from Japan, Norway, Africa, Portugal and Chile.

These reserves continue to support the professional scrimshanders of Nantucket, New Bedford, Boston, Hawaii and other places where a local traffic in whale teeth remains within the law. In areas where such traffic is unlawful, the work continues legally, if pursued as a hobby, or if commissioned to be done on a whale tooth provided by the buyer, in which case only a service is bought and sold, not the material.

There has also been a considerable impact on the antique scrimshaw market. The law as it exists at this writing makes no qualification for age. Antique work has been withdrawn from many normal markets, including most of the large auction houses. It is too impractical for an auctioneer to have to verify the intrastate origins of individual pieces of scrimshaw, and too dangerous not to.

A recent Bourne catalogue of marine items contained an insert announcing the withdrawal of scrimshaw from the auction block until such time as the law could be "... amended so that any items made of body parts of the whale that were in the country at the time of the passage of the law may be sold. If you are interested, please write your senator and representative . . ."

All the collectors, scrimshanders and merchants who for whatever reasons favor an amendment to the law point to the absurdity of making illegal something which is so

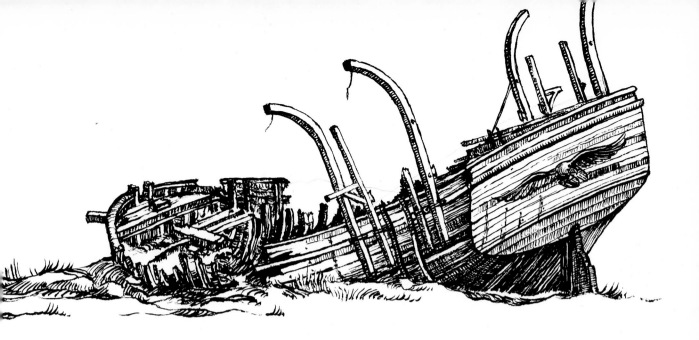

obviously after the fact. "What do they expect us to do, put the teeth back into the mouth of the whale?"

The rebuttal to this is expressed by those who feel the continued use of body parts of endangered creatures continues to stimulate interest, therefore perpetuating the demand.

Obviously true, but where a demand exists, it cannot be eliminated, only suppressed. Supression stimulates the very interest and demand it was intended to eliminate. In this case, a black market is created, along with higher values and the expensive necessity for enforcing laws leading to more laws in an endless chain. This is the double bind.

What can be done? That which can be done for the whales has been done, at least by the United States. This nation has stopped whaling, banned import or export of whale products entirely, and urges the same course on the other nations that have not. If these measures continue to be enforced, it is the ultimate effort a sovereign nation can practically make.

It seems unnecessary to sacrifice a living folk art, scrimshaw, when there is nothing to be gained by its loss. The art can be allowed life by the free exchange of material already on hand, until such time as the extinction or survival of the whales is decided, possibly along with the extinction or survival of man himself.

I do not know of one scrimshander who quibbles with the concept of protecting the whales. The whale commands our respect. It is a respect very deeply felt, tracing back into those dim times when we adorned ourselves with the teeth of the beasts we hunted and ate, many of which in turn hunted and ate us — the respect for a worthy adversary. The whale was unquestionably the noblest. This respect is akin to love, and it lingers not fleetingly in the fickle brain, but in the blood.

Why are the teeth of whales necessary to the preservation of scrimshaw as an art form? This book is the best answer I am able to make, pitifully inadequate as it seems in its two dimensions, for this paper cannot be ivory.

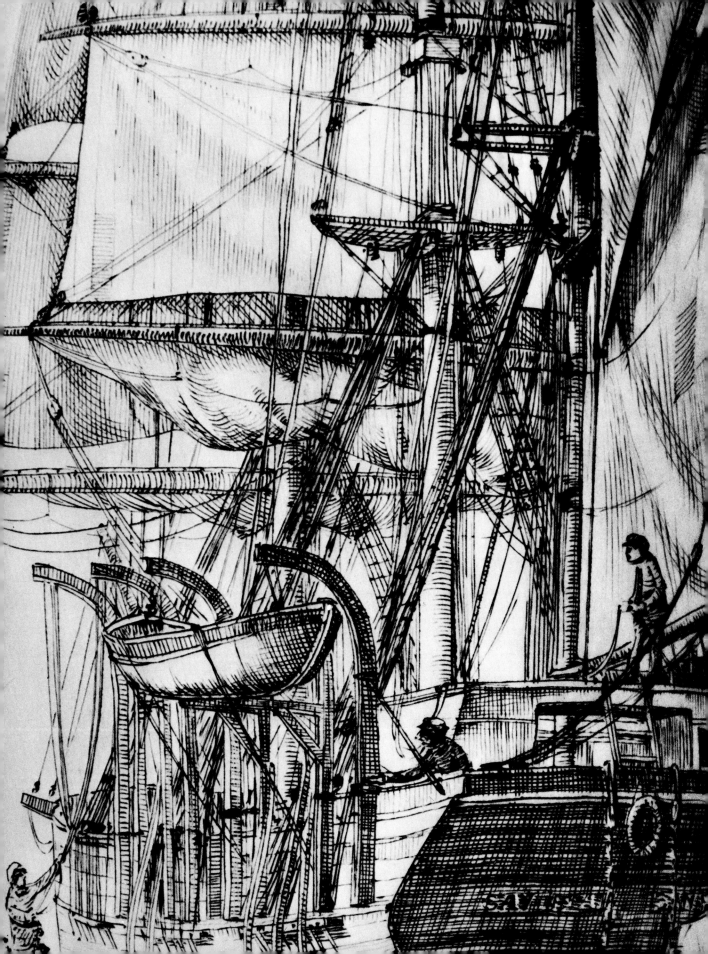

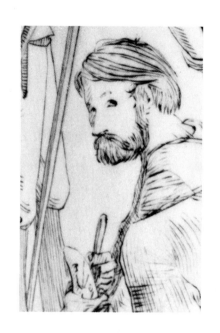

SCRIMSHAW

by

Wm. Gilkerson

A Photographic Portfolio

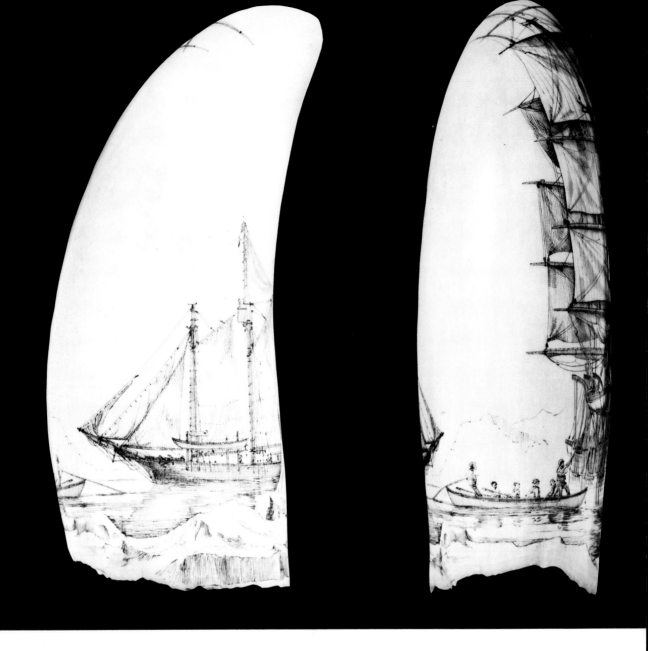

IV Whalers

What distinguished the whaling vessel from her contemporaries? Within, massive timbers, strength (see page 51) and the capacity for a big cargo of oil; without, bluff lines, plain rig and an inventory of specialized gear, much of it illustrated in these views of a tooth scrimshaw'd with the bark *Gay Head* and the schooner *Lettitia* together in polar ice, drying their sails.

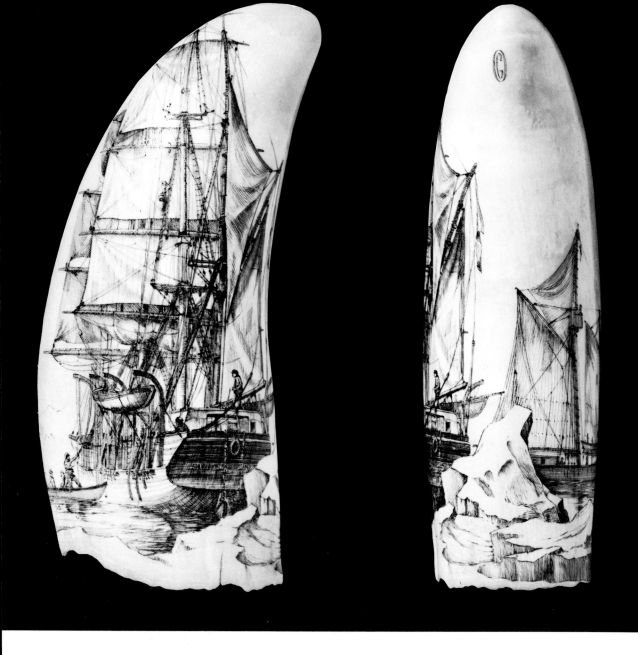

Notable whale ship features were their davits and boats, their masthead hoops (*Lettitia's* lookout station was partially enclosed), and the hurricane house on larger vessels — *Gay Head's* shows clearly — two deckhouses joined overhead with the helm between them. The starboard house contained the galley, to port were lockers. Not in view here are the brick furnaces with their iron try-pots, or the skids over the decks with their extra boats.

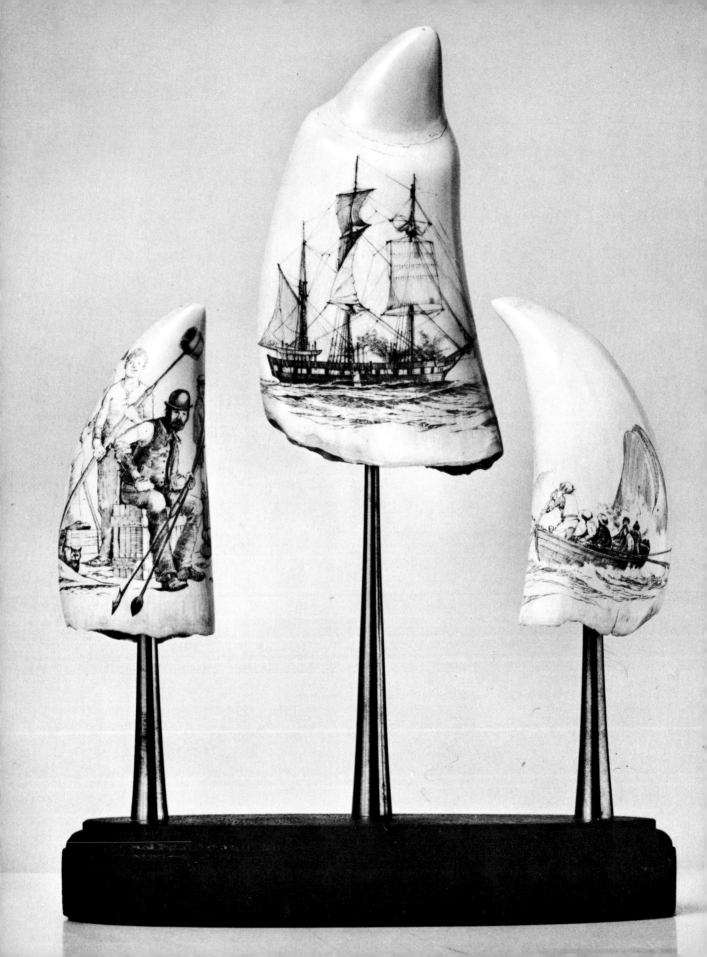

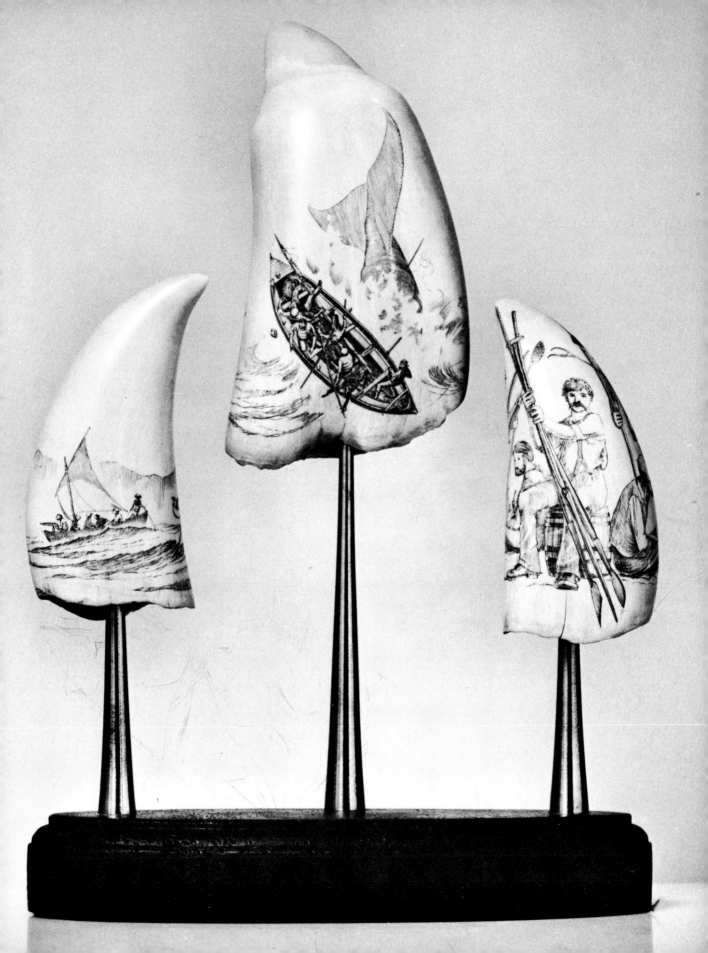

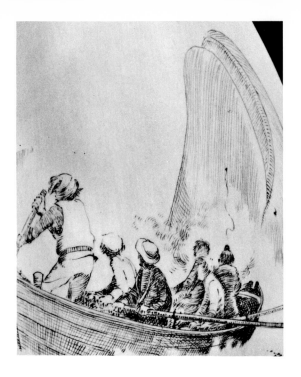

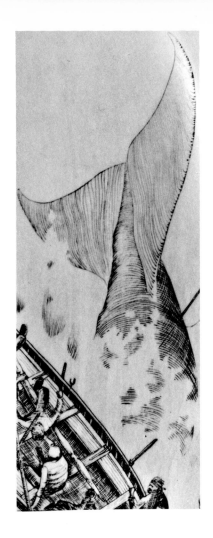

CALIFORNIA GRAY whale breaches, smoke billows from the bows of the whaleboat as the harpooner fires a bomb lance from point-blank range. Above detail is from the right hand piece on page 44. This tooth is one of three, all depicting whaling scenes from the northwest coast. The set is shown front on page 44 and reverse on page 45.

The middle piece of the set depicts two sperm whaling scenes: the mother ship, a small whaling bark, is hove to and cutting in, her tryworks smoking. On the opposite face, a harpooned whale sounds, giving the whaleboat a thump on his way down (see detail, this page). For one instant before capsizing, the boat hangs suspended on a lather of foam.

The third piece overleaf illustrates implements of whaling. At the left, the harpooner holds a toggle harpoon and the killing lance, behind him a youth stands with the bailer. To the right, a seated crewman displays bone spade (L), boarding knife (M) and cutting spade (R). Just visible above and behind him are the blubber fork and the skimmer. He is flanked by two figures

seated on the ground: to his left, the scrimshander (see detail, page 41) and to his right the sailmaker (see detail, right).

Small boats, such as the one in the detail, upper right, fished for gray whales during the late 19th century, putting out from shore stations along the California coast. They carried the usual boat's equipment, plus a bomb gun in the bow. Whaling for the California gray was called "devil fishing." Although easier than his cousins to locate because of his seasonal migrations between Mexico and the arctic, the gray was unpredictable when speared and frequently dangerous. This led to many a yarn.

Naturalist Charles M. Scammon, in his

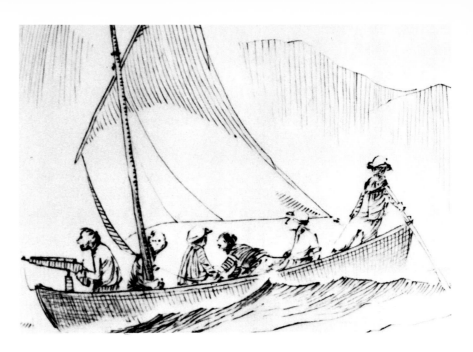

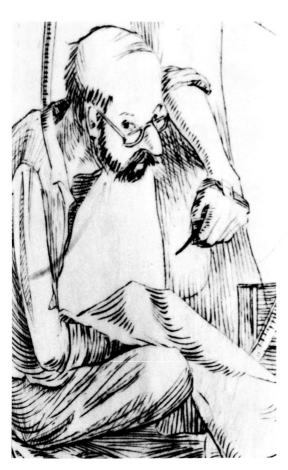

classic *Marine Mammals of the North-western Coast* published in 1874, reports the following conversation between a whale ship master and his first mate, a man more used to sperm whales than the grays:

(The mate) "I shipped to this ship to go a whalin' . . . why, cap'n, these here critters in this bay ain't whales."

"Well, if they ain't whales, what are they?" asked the captain, in a husky voice.

"Well," replied the mate, "I don't know rightly what they be, but I hev a strong notion they are a cross 'tween a sea serpent and an alligator. Why, these mussel-diggers will turn round in their tracks, Cap'n; and it's no use . . . you can't git these here Ripsacks without a good deal of boat-stavin' . . ."

Turning and attacking his attacker was a favorite maneuver of a speared gray. One skipper who experienced this told Scammon of it as follows:

"I sung out to the men to pull for the shore as they loved their lives; and when that boat struck the beach, we scattered. I'll admit I never stopped to look round; but the Boat steerer yelled out: 'Cap'n, the old whale is after us still,' when I told all hands to climb trees!"

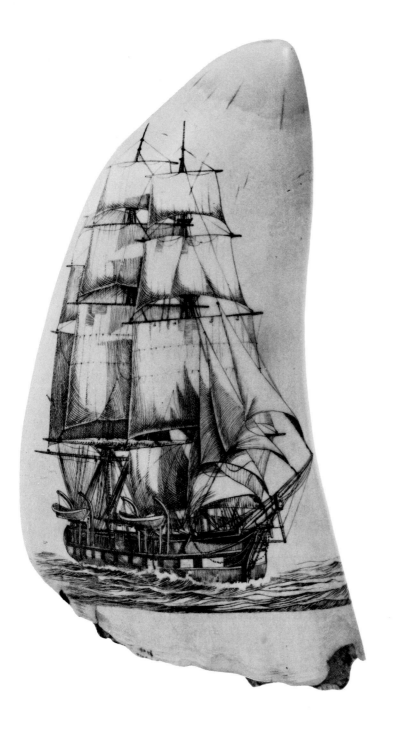

THE LAST of the old Yankee whale ships still afloat is the bark Charles W. Morgan, *here shown in two phases of her career. Built in New Bedford in 1841,* Morgan *fished for 80 years, made 37 voyages, took over 2,500 whales, brought in more than 75,000 barrels of oil. She has been aground, witnessed mutinies, weathered hurricanes, been struck thrice by lightning, and was once set afire by her crew. Also, she is probably the most scrimshaw'd ship ever.*

*HER SAILING career ended
with a film role in 1921,*
Down to the Sea in Ships,
*for which she was fitted as
she was then thought to have
been in her early career, as
a full-rigged ship with
single tops'ls and white gun
stripe, black ports. She
appears thus fitted, (left).
In 1941,* Morgan *was towed to
Mystic, Conn., made a museum
ship, restored to bark rig
with split tops'ls and
plain black sides, right.*

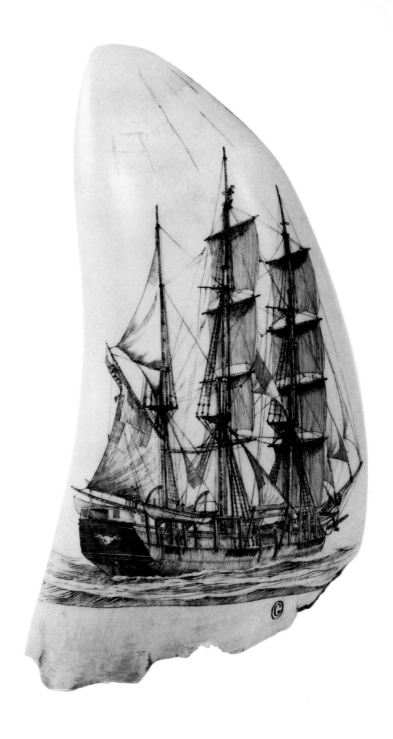

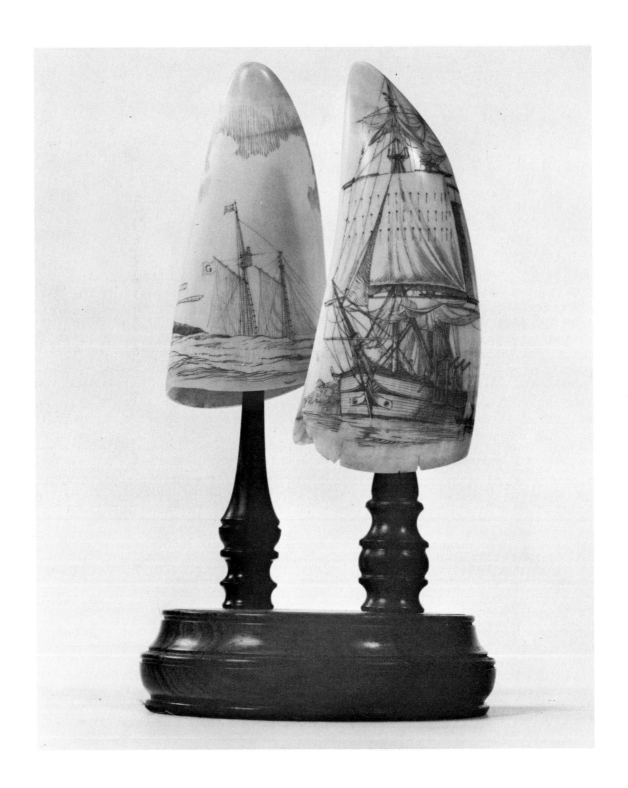

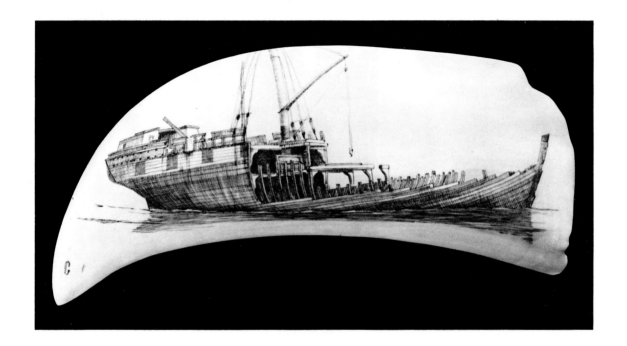

The bones of a sea hawk are scrimshaw'd above, plucked by harpies of the shore. The whaler *California* made her last voyage in 1906, shortly thereafter she ended her career on the mud in Oakland, California, as depicted above from an old photograph. She was dismantled, piece by piece, for the still-valuable material in her. There was much of it, even after 70 years of hard service, for whalers were the strongest vessels afloat. They needed real muscle to stay at sea for years, repeatedly absorbing the wrenching strains of cutting tackle and fluke chains in choppy seas. An idea of the abuses these ships routinely endured is given firsthand by Frank T. Bullen in his *Cruise of the Cachalot:*

> *"It was dark before we got our prize secured by the fluke-chain, so that we could not commence operations before morning. That night it blew hard, and we got an idea of the strain these vessels are sometimes subjected to. Sometimes the ship rolled one way and the whale the other, being divided by a big sea, the wrench at the fluke-chain, as the two masses fell apart down different hollows, making the vessel quiver from truck to keelson as if she was being torn asunder. Then we would come together again with a crash and a shock that almost threw everybody out of their bunks. Many an earnest prayer did I breathe . . ."*

These heavily timbered, well-fastened ships outlasted by decades the merchantmen which were their contemporaries.

On the opposite page, a pair of scrimshaw'd teeth depict two small whalers, a schooner (masts visible) and a brig, becalmed, tryworks in action.

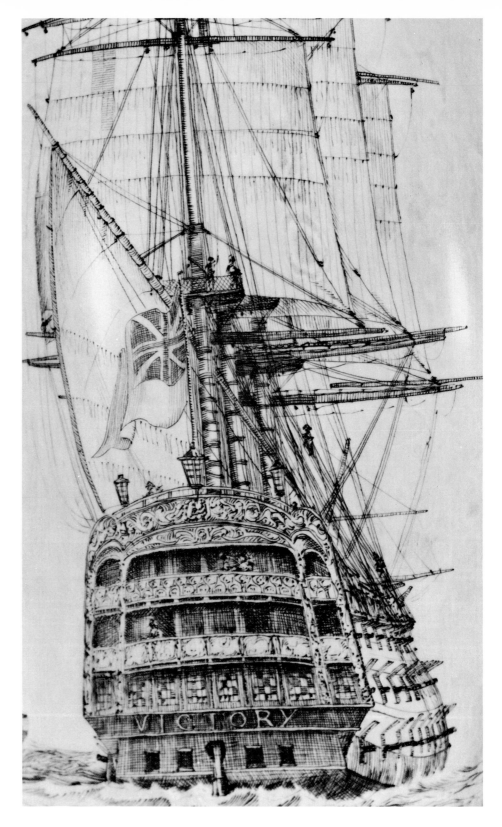

Detail from page 55

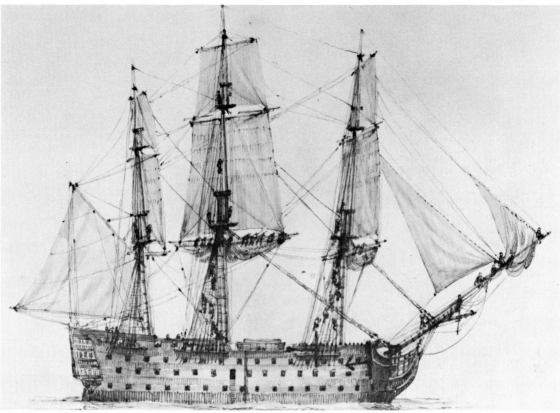

PENCIL and watercolor is a preliminary study for the engravings on pages 54 and 55.

V Ship Portraits

What is this growing fascination with the old, dead sailing ships? Does it represent a desperate nostalgia for a kind of machinery which men could build and operate with their hands, and upon which they could float free — free and without reliance on an electronic technology with its hum of hidden machinery and crucial rows of tiny buttons to push and plastic knobs to twist? Perhaps.

By the end of the last century, man's ships had flowered, and the ultimate word in hewn timber, spun hemp, hammered iron, and sewn cotton had been spoken. The clippers and the down-Easters and the Whalers and all the others embodied the accumulated knowledge of countless builders over countless centuries — and of the sailors, millions upon millions of anonymous seamen who toiled away their lives under sail in ships, blown by the wind on which their stories are written.

> *"They mark our passage as a race of men.*
> *We shall not see such ships as those again."*

That sounds ever so much better than if Mr. Masefield had aimed for accuracy rather than rhetoric, in which case he would have written: "We shall not see very many such ships as those again, relatively speaking." There are a few of the old windships left. They even seem to be making something of a comeback.

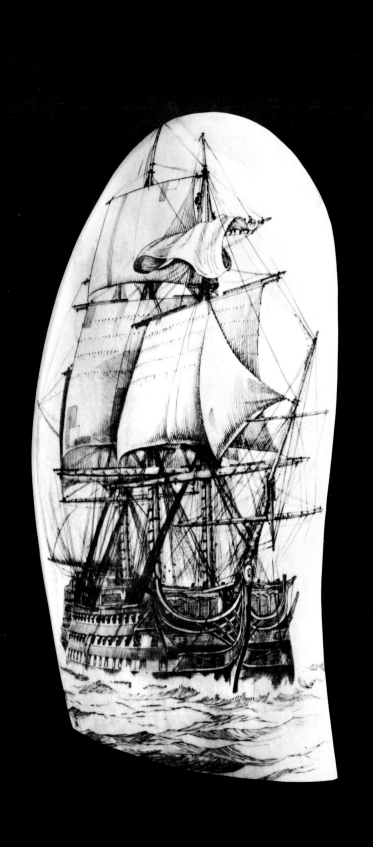

H.M.S. VICTORY *thumps along in a freshening breeze, foam churning under her massive, bluff bows, lower ports closed and t'gallant sails furling. Face of this large whale tooth depicts the big warship as she was painted and rigged in 1805 when she served as Nelson's flag ship at Trafalgar. By that time she was already an old ship, in and out of retirement, rebuilt and modernized. This piece was done from draft, photos, and sketches in her Portsmouth berth.*

REVERSE side of piece shows Victory *as she was when launched in 1765, before later modifications. Open stern galleries were decorated with elaborate carvings and gilt work. Two figures stand in the upper gallery, likely the flag captain with his secretary. On the next level down, a solitary figure broods, possibly Keppel, Admiral of the channel fleet in 1778, meditating on the depredations of raider John Paul Jones, on the loose in the Channel.*

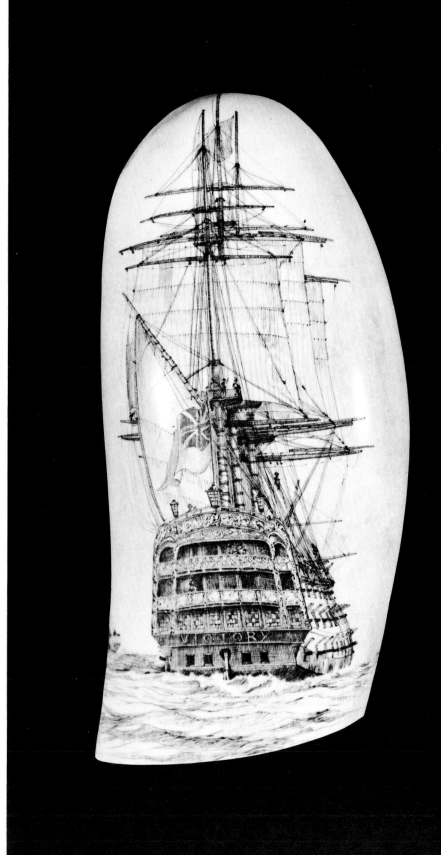

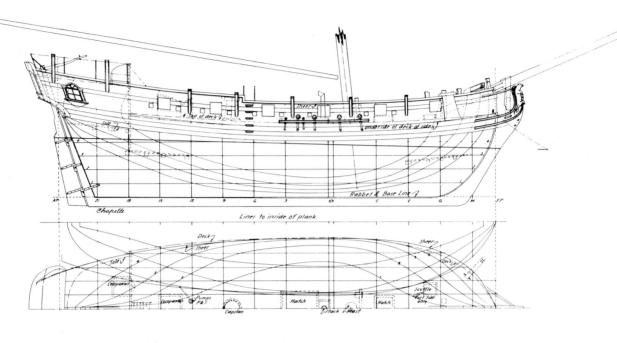

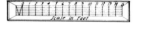

There are the museum ships — the historical ships which have survived. In the case of a few old warships, there has been a reluctance to dispose of them because they so distinguished themselves in battle. This is the case with *H.M.S. Victory* (see pages 54, 55) a ship so old she was already elderly when America's most famous survivor, the U.S. Frigate *Constitution* (see pages 58 through 61), was launched in 1797. The most ancient of the lot, Sweden's *Wasa* (see page 65) sank soon after her launching in 1628 and was raised again after some three and a half centuries, to be restored in Stockholm where a special museum now houses her.

Still other old ships have been meticulously duplicated in full-sized replica. Most of the original square rigged vessels that still float date from the late 1800's, and they owe their survival to the superb initial construction, the craftsmanship and material, which has permitted them to outlast their own obsolescence until, like the design on the Smith Bros. Cough Drops package, they became fashionable, and therefore useful, again — as museums rather than cargo-carriers. Examples illustrated in these pages include *Charles W. Morgan* (see pages 48-49), *Balclutha* (see pages 109-111) and the scow schooner *Alma* (see page 64).

There are many, many others, and still more are being newly built by old methods. All offer themselves as living models for any illustrator of old time ships.

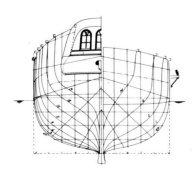

56

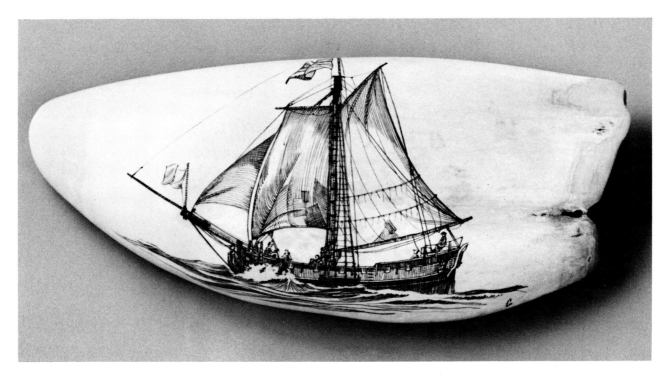

LINES of sloop Ferrett, *on opposite page, preserved from an old Admiralty draft, made possible the scrimshaw profile of the vessel illustrated above.*

They are natural to the medium of scrimshaw, not only in the traditional sense, because it was on decks such as those that the whole art form flourished, but beyond tradition. The tracery of their slender wooden spars and rigging makes a brittle, intricate pattern which is suggestive of engraving when seen in life against the sky. And the lines and strakes of a wooden hull when cut into a smooth ivory surface with a knife suggest the hewn form of the ship supported in water.

The compatibility of square riggers and scrimshaw seems to be heightened by accuracy of detail in a ship engraving, and usually weakened by inaccuracy. An inaccurately-wrought ship that pretends to accuracy never quite makes it, even if it is clever. And nothing is more embarrassing than an unclever pretense. The only alternatives, then, seem to be either a regard for accuracy, or a total disregard, which can in some cases create a pleasing primitive effect.

I am drawn to accuracy, and to that end have had the advantage of the better part of a lifetime in, around, on and under various sailing vessels. In these circumstances a feeling develops for how all the little strings and bits and pieces work, and how the sails flap and fold and how the water splashes.

This has all been very helpful in a general way, but a ship portrait also demands a specific knowledge of detail. It has been said a ship is like a woman, sometimes better. That's as may be, but it is certainly true of both that no two look alike. The details of hull and rigging in the depiction of a sailing ship are like the lines and contours, the facial musculature of an individual in the portrait of a person, and anyone who thinks all clippers look alike, or whalers, or frigates, or lumber schoon-

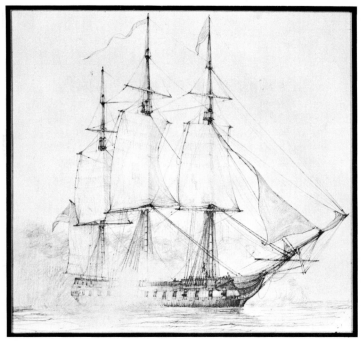

OLD IRONSIDES *fires a salvo — study for engravings.*

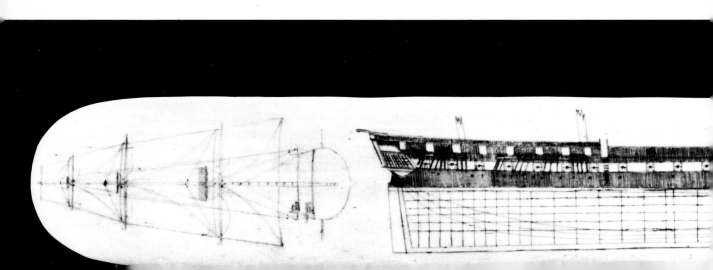

ers, or whatever, hasn't looked for a moment at any of them. And so the ship portrait is as challenging as the portraits of a lovely woman.

Fortunately there is a great deal of graphic reference material available so that just about any ship can be studied in detail. If the lines of a ship are available, the eye can duplicate her three-dimensionally. A ship's lines show her in cross section at various stations, as well as in vertical section, side and bottom, in such a way as to reveal her form. The little scrimshaw of the sloop *Ferrett* on page 57 was done from the lines shown on page 56. This is a simple profile, but much more complicated angles are possible. Most of the old warships on these pages, such as *Victory, Wasa,* and *Constitution* were done from line plans. *Constitution's* lines as such are depicted as the subject of an engraving illustrated below.

Marine historian Howard Chapelle has done many books on sailing craft and filled them with line plans. Such works are indispensible. In the back of this book is a list including these and other reference works which are invaluable in ship illustrating.

Sometimes hull lines for a certain ship are available, but no rigging plan. In that case it's necessary to make an educated guess, and the rigging standard to a vessel of that type is used. Sometimes reconstruction of a ship is very difficult, as in the case of the ships on the front and back covers of this book, and in detail on page 62: *Bon-Homme Richard* and *Serapis,* on the reverse, the Continental Frigate *Alliance.*

In a night battle, John Paul Jones in *BonHomme Richard* fought the *Serapis,* a greatly superior vessel, and won, with less than no help from the *Alliance* which was commanded by a mad and mutinous French captain. During the action, Jones, seemingly beaten and invited to surrender, uttered his now famous "I have not yet begun to fight," and it is at this moment that the battle is depicted, with the two principal ships lashed bow to stern, *Serapis* anchored and sails aback.

The problem in designing the piece was that nobody really knows what any of these ships looked like, although there are some clues. *BonHomme Richard* was built in 1760 in France to serve in that country's East India trade under her original name, *Duc de Duras.* We know her dimen-

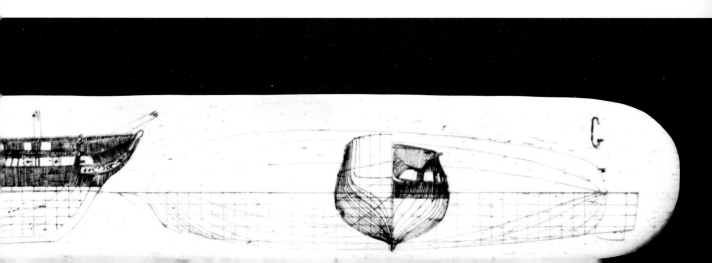

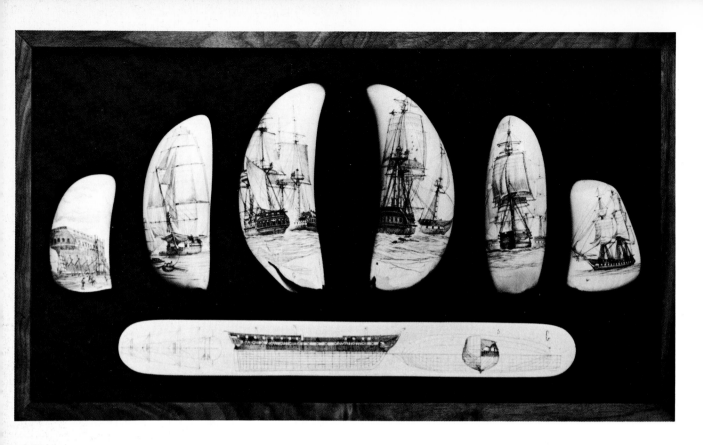

FRIGATE CONSTITUTION *is depicted in various phases of her long career in this cased set of six matched teeth and one bone busk. From right to left,* Constitution *(a) is under construction, on the ways at Hartt's Shipyard, Boston, 1796; (b) escapes a pursuing British squadron in a calm by kedging and towing; (c) defeats H.M. Frigate* Guerriere; *(d) defeats H.M. Frigate* Java; *(e) defeats H.M. Frigate* Cyane *and H.M. War Sloop* Levant; *(f) lies peacefully at anchor. Her lines are reproduced on the whalebone busk at the bottom. The legendary ship still floats, is fondly remembered for giving the British lion's tail more tweaks than any other ship in the fledgling U.S. Navy. Cannonballs bouncing off her green timbers earned her the nickname "Old Ironsides." These pieces were prepared from plans, photos, and from life.*

sions because Jones recorded them in his journal; we know how many cannon she mounted, that she was painted black and a few other details, but not enough to give a historian any really comprehensive picture of the ship.

The few models of her in various institutions were built in recent times, and no two are alike. Some have glaring inaccuracies. Paintings of the *BonHomme Richard,* old and new, also suffer from inaccuracy.

There is not much to do in such a situation except make the most learned guess possible, but in this case a happy accident took place. While thumbing through a book of reproductions of marine graphics, I encountered a beautiful vintage painting from England's Greenwich Maritime Museum portraying in profile a big British East Indiaman, the *Princess Royal,* a contemporary ship with *BonHomme Richard.*

The name *Princess Royal* sent me back to an account of the *Richard-Serapis* battle. Just prior to the battle, Jones was flying British colors, attempting to delay the fight as he maneuvered for the most favorable position possible. He was hailed by Captain Pearson of *Serapis,* who demanded he identify his ship.

"This is the *Princess Royal,*" Jones responded.

The ship in the reproduction matches

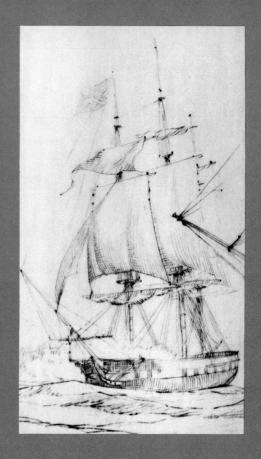

H.M. WAR SLOOP LEVANT *plunges, powder smoke billows as gunners maintain a cannonade. The detail above shows the reverse face of (e) on the opposite page, here greatly enlarged. In actual size, this engraving fits on a postage stamp. Below, detail from (c).*

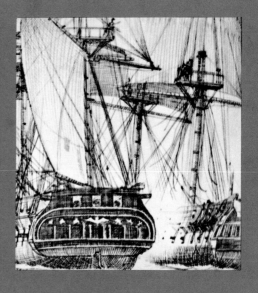

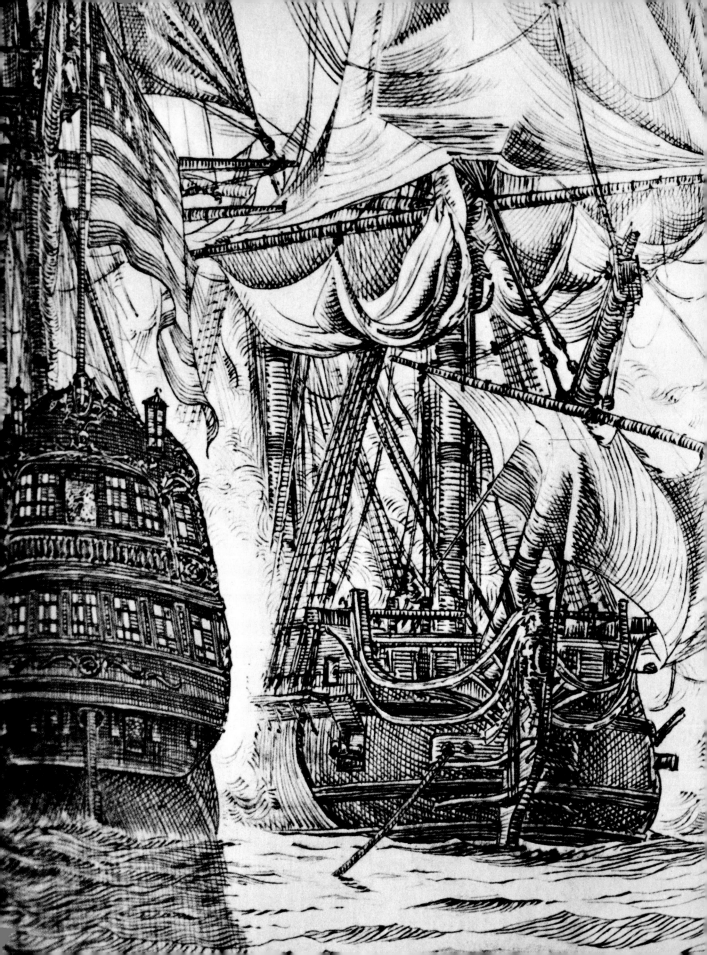

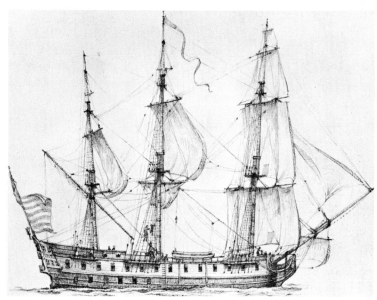

descriptions of *BonHomme Richard,* is almost exactly the same dimensions and tonnage, and about the same rig. It seems safe to assume she was also of the same general appearance, for it stands to reason the cagey Jones would choose for his masquerade an existing vessel which actually resembled *Richard.*

So here was a very valuable discovery. By modifying the ship shown in the period painting to incorporate the features known to have belonged to *Richard,* a reconstruction became possible, shown above, a pencil drawing of her in profile. With this drawing as reference, it was possible to pose her as illustrated, perhaps looking in this tiny engraving very much like her real self.

We'll never know. She was sunk during the action, and Jones shifted himself and what was left of his decimated crew over to *Serapis.* The depiction of *Serapis* was also a guess, but not a very chancy one, for *Serapis* was one of a class of vessels of which much is known. *Alliance,* on the back cover, was no guess at all, because she was sister ship to a vessel whose lines survive intact, and they were available.

Fortunately, ship portraits are not usually so demanding as these of *Bon-Homme Richard* and *Serapis.*

I am sometimes asked to what extent I have been influenced by old scrimshaw and if I copy designs. As to influence, it was the traditional notion of portraying my own vessel on a whale tooth which got me started scrimshanding — on a tooth that was given me by a big friend who is a bouncer and bartender in a North Beach saloon.

It was my first adventure with the art form. I used my own style, portraying the

BELOW: Catboat Andy *zips along with a reef in, wind abeam, spray blowing.*
RIGHT: Scow schooner Alma *of San Francisco with towering deckload of hay bales, headed downriver. Recalls an ex-scow-hand of river sailing: "You could just come around, tack, and come around immediately again, or your bowsprit would be caught amongst the trees."*

OPPOSITE PAGE, ABOVE: Front and reverse of a tooth depicting Swedish Royal Ship Wasa *wearing the sails under which she capsized and sank on her maiden voyage, 1628. Today she has been raised and housed in Stockholm's Wasa Museum.*

OPPOSITE PAGE, BELOW: Danish ketch Fri, *a typical small Baltic trader, now a yacht; mounted on a plaque carved from her own sternboard.*

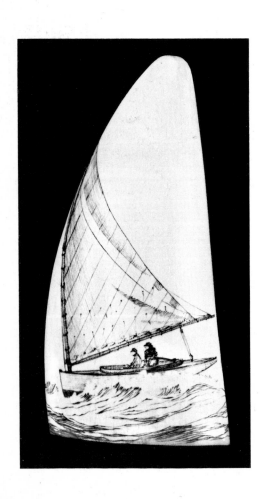

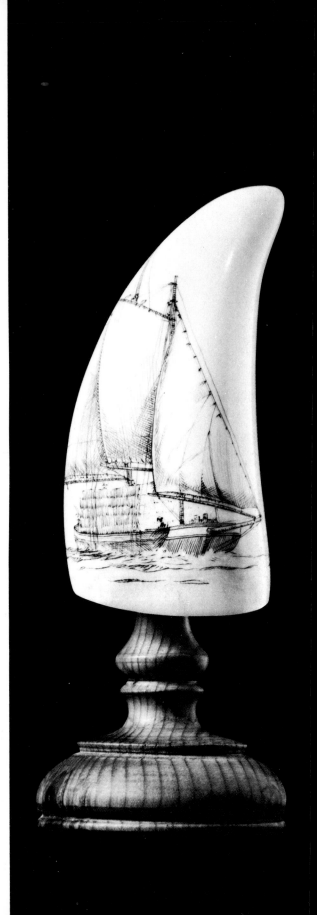

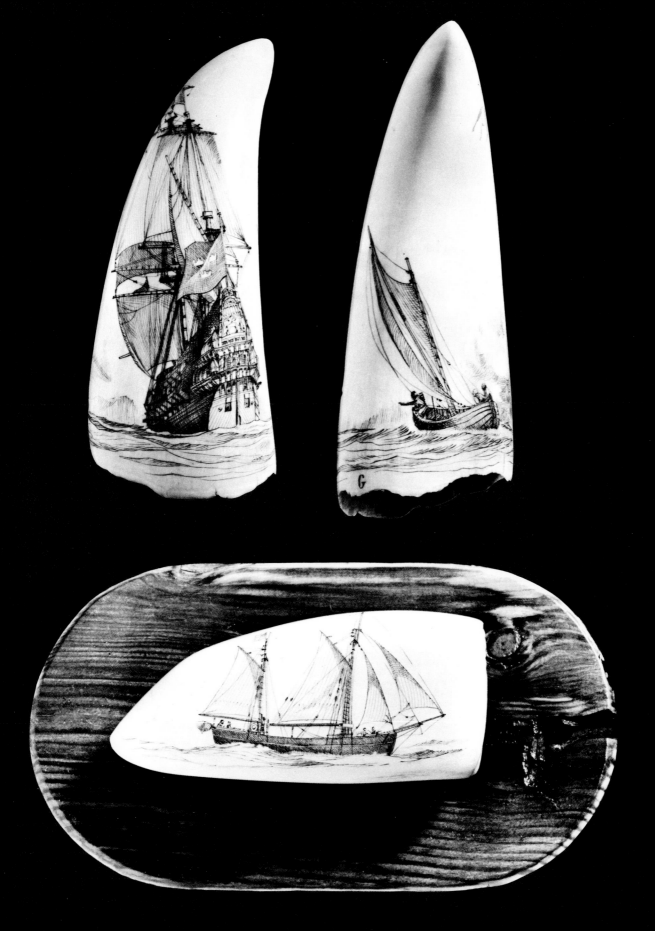

BELOW: Motor Yacht Seaplay *of Atlanta, scrimshaw'd whale tooth in walnut casket. Executed from a series of pencil drawings of the actual vessel, made while bobbing around in the middle of a crowded harbor; not the easiest way to prepare a ship portrait.*

OPPOSITE PAGE, ABOVE: 1914 steam tug Eppleton Hall. *Scott Newhall purchased her from a breaker's yard in Newcastle on Tyne, England, where she lay condemned, listing, stripped of fittings, decks burned out, filling with each flood tide, emptying with the ebb. Story of her restoration and trip to San Francisco under her own steam is told in the book* Eppleton Hall *written by Newhall. Scrimshaw prepared from photos and life.*

OPPOSITE PAGE, BELOW: Model steam launch Belle, *a scrimshaw'd elephant ivory plaque. This engraving was made from a model in the San Francisco Maritime Museum.*

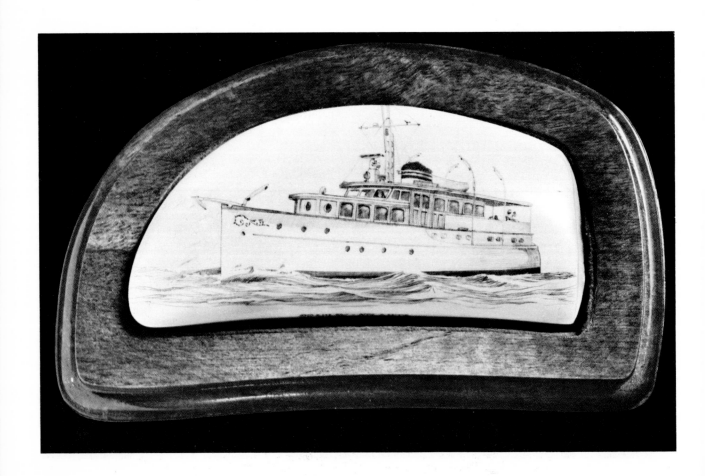

66

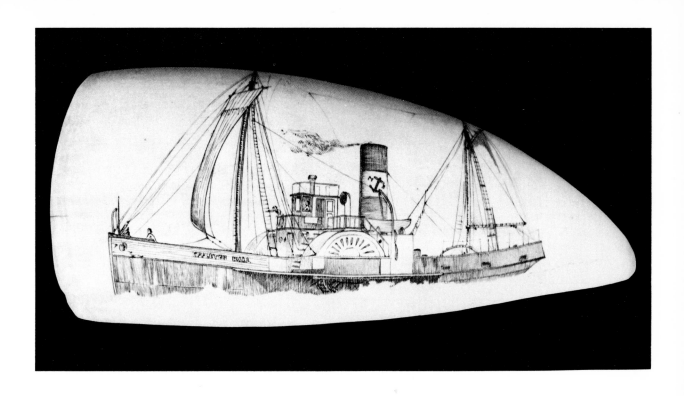

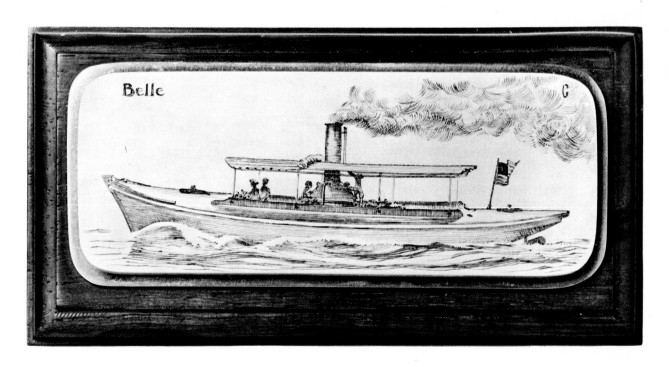

67

and so I tacked to come down for
S'Gravenhage. On this tack the
tiller broke again. We shipped still
another tiller and re-assumed our course
E until coming within 1/4 mile of the
coast - between S'Gravenhage and
Katwik an Zee - where we again
dropped anchor - with 60 metres of
slept last night.
we found the wind
pletely S. and increased
We attempted to
but it is fast on the
weather reports heavy
coast, so I have de-
here until tomorrow
onditions may be
think that our jury-
up to handling a
of any force (if I
jmuiden), but we
d chance to fetch
the wind either
back to E. I am
the anchor chain
nditions.
rvals that we are
in 4 fathoms of

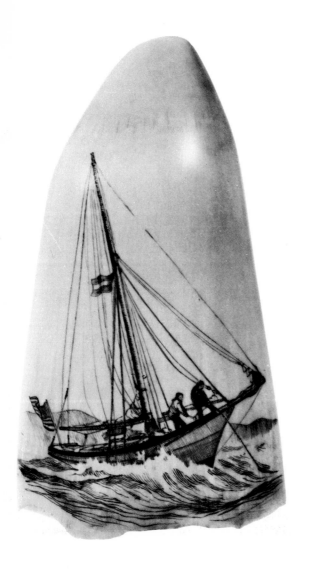

03

1400 HOURS   Berthed next to fishing boat in 1st harbor.

This morning another attempt was made to raise the anchor - in vain. The wind had, however, backed again to SE, and, despite its force (gale 7-8), I felt that we could beat down to this place. We cut the hawse chain and made sail. The storm jib which had held during our fight finally split, but we brought her into the wind under the old mainsail (double-reefed) and the storm trisail which we'd jury-rigged onto the jib boom. The improvised tiller finally held, and we made it in here on two long and two short tacks.

Our condition, the condition of the ship, and the condition of all gear on board is lamentable. A rough list of the damage sustained includes:

4 sails split
halliard carried away
jib sheets worn through
dinghy lost
cabin table ripped from deck
steel tiller bar broken

all clothing wet-dirty
fenders lost overboard
anchor lost
6 metres anchor chain lost

104

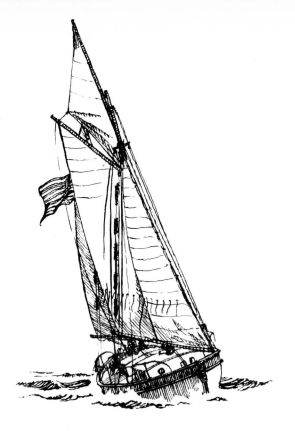

pose of her that appears in a photo from Scott Newhall's book *Eppleton Hall.* Generally I do not copy simply because it's less interesting than making up the whole thing to suit myself. Photos are very useful for visual reference. The photographs of *Lettitia* and *Gay Head* (see pages 20 and 21) were invaluable to the accurate portrayal of those vessels (see pages 42 and 43).

Some working drawings, or studies, for finished engravings are included in this collection, mostly profile views for maximum detail. On a finished piece I try to show two views of the vessel being portrayed. In the case of *H.M.S. Victory,* the bow view (see page 54) depicts the vessel as she was rigged and painted in 1805, at the time of the Battle of Trafalgar, whereas her stern view (see page 55) shows her before her remodelling, or as she appeared when she was launched in 1765.

Ship models are delightful to work from when available. Then the artist can choose his pose and get the entire perspective he wants of the ship in a way that is impossible from flat plans or photos, or even from the actual vessel herself. Little *Belle* on page 67 is a model portrait, and refer-

boat as realistically as possible, and I have worked that way ever since. Almost all the engravings I've done are of my conception and design, with a few exceptions.

I have copied photos, although infrequently. The engraving of *Eppleton Hall* (see page 67) is more or less a copy of a

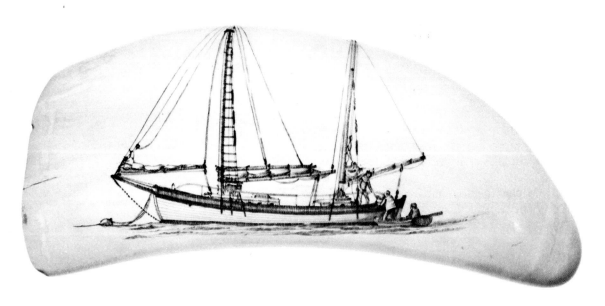

ence was made to a model in preparing the *Constitution* set.

Working from the actual vessel would seem to be the most desirable approach to a portrait, but a real ship also presents major difficulties. If the ship is of any appreciable size and tied up at a dock, her image is distorted to the eye unless she is viewed from a considerable distance. If she is encountered in movement, she will soon be past, faster than the pencil can capture her details.

Small yachts can be viewed at fairly close quarters without perspective distortion. A number of yachts appear in these pages, even a large, luxurious power vessel, which crinkles the nose of some sail purists, but which was an interesting challenge for me as a project, even though my choice of subjects is obviously more inclined toward sail.

I find many yachts as inspiring to engrave as big square riggers. Also small working boats. My own first vessel, *Cutlass,* is illustrated on page 68 in a predicament off the Dutch coast in a gale. The same vessel appears on page 73 as she was re-rigged a year later. Originally named *Kalliope,* she was built in Sweden in 1896 and still survives. My subsequent yacht, the gaff ketch *Griffyn,* appears in various views on pages 70 and 71.

Depicting a small vessel allows its crew to be shown, even their faces sometimes. This can add great warmth and reality to a piece in a way that is impossible in treatments of larger, nobler ships. There is a special charm to the little ships in this miniature medium, where a great spreading mural occupies no more than a few square inches.

If Michelangelo had been a scrimshander, he could have carried his entire Sistine ceiling away with him in his pocket.

GRIFFYN — *Gaff-rigged 18-ton Hannah-design Carol ketch which the artist sailed and lived aboard for years has been a favorite scrimshaw subject. In lower right she is running, jibing the mizzen. In upper left she is shown in an ink-study close-hauled under tops'l, and in lower left at anchor, receiving visitors.*

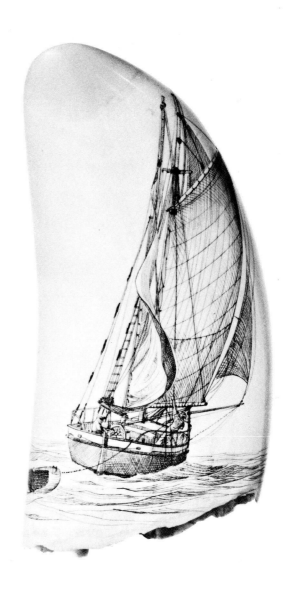

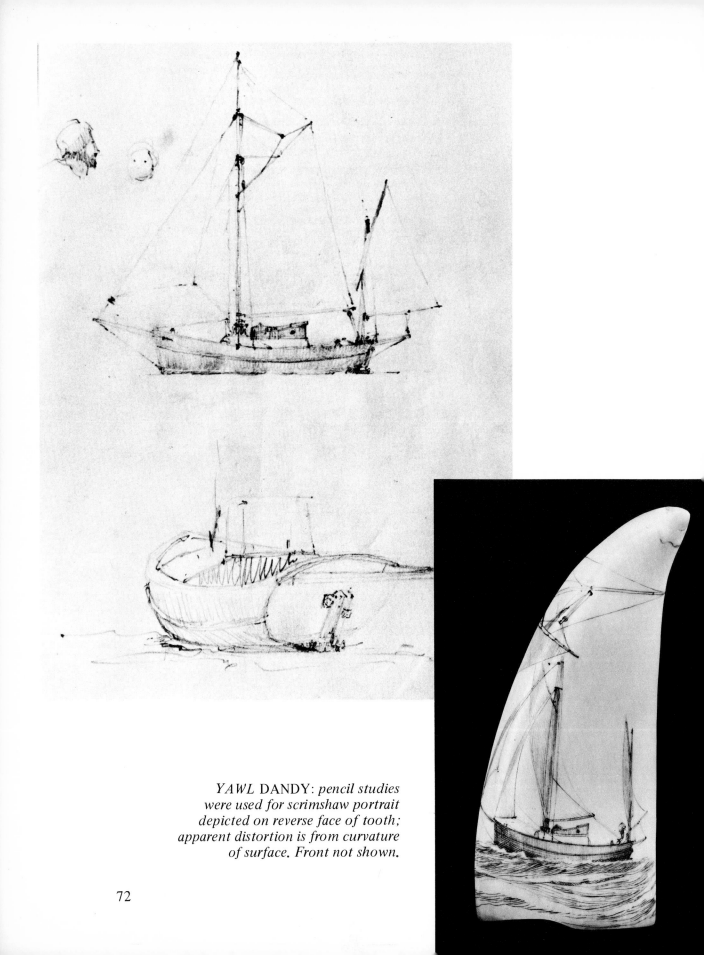

YAWL DANDY: *pencil studies were used for scrimshaw portrait depicted on reverse face of tooth; apparent distortion is from curvature of surface. Front not shown.*

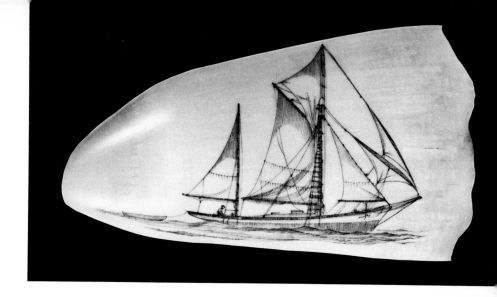

KETCH CUTLASS, *a 50-ft. Scandinavian racing yacht built in 1896 as* Kalliope. *She was the author's first boat, appearing above with the rig given her during northern European-British Isles cruise, 1961-62. Earlier on this voyage she retained her original cutter rig, as on page 68 (reverse face of the above piece) set against pages of her log describing the incident.*

WHITES OF EYES: *"Depicting a small boat allows its crew to be shown, even their faces . . ."*

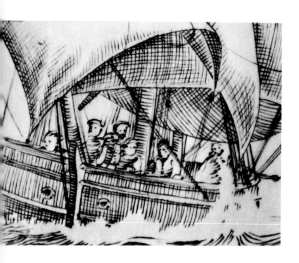

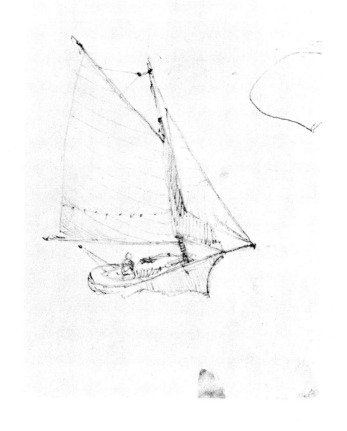

FRIENDSHIP SLOOP *is portrayed in quick pencil sketch made between maneuvers during a regatta. Thumbnail drawings such as this one (right) from life capture feeling of vessel, accuracy is later gleaned from plans.*

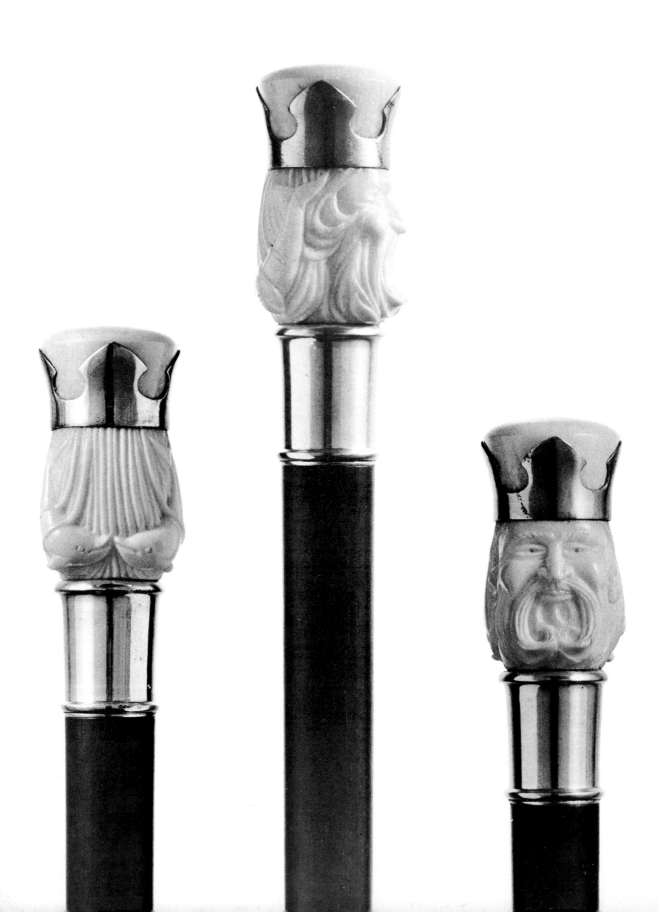

VI The Crafted Artifact

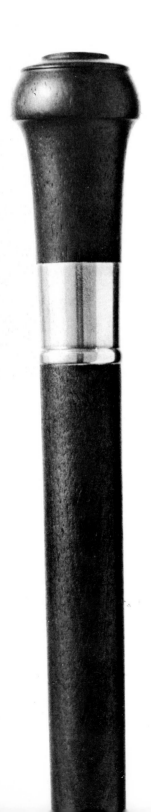

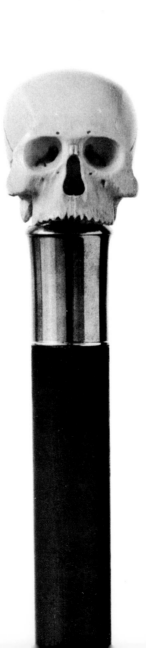

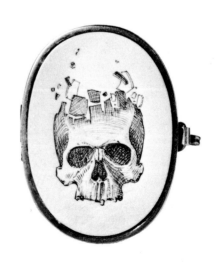

OVERLEAF: On page 74, Father Neptune in his benevolent aspect appears on the head of a walking stick, carved in walrus ivory. Dolphins play through his hair. Crown and ferrule are silver, shaft is of Brazilian rosewood. On page 75, rough drawing and plan for the piece from the artist's notebook.

WALKING STICK, (far left); rosewood head with ivory bead, louro preto shaft, brass ferrule; 2nd left — walking stick with elephant ivory skull head, bronze ferrules, rosewood shaft. Left center — a small silver snuff box with African elephant ivory plaque engraved with exploding skull. Opposite page shows two views of a walrus ivory carving depicting an allegorical three-faced head, a bagpipe bag clasp ornament on silver plaque.

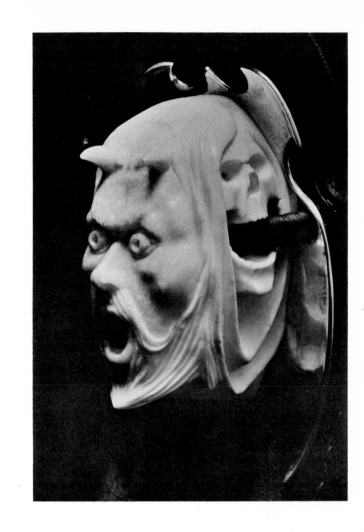

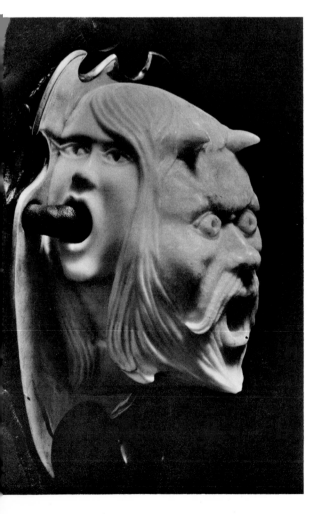

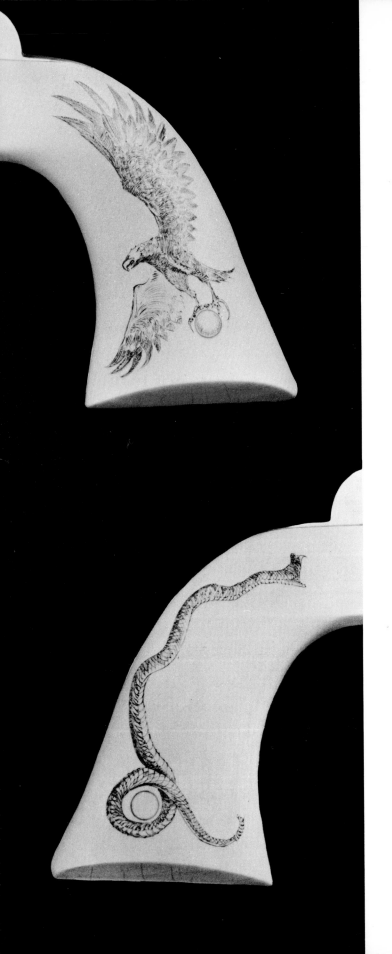

COLT NAVY *percussion revolver,*
in a rosewood case with
grips and powder flask of
scrimshaw'd elephant ivory.
Depicted are five predatory
kinds of creatures — the bird
kingdom represented by the eagle;
the reptile kingdom, by a
striking diamond-back rattler;
the predatory under-sea
creatures by a hammerhead
shark; the four-legged
mammals by a running wolf (opp.
face of flask, not shown); and
insects by a black widow spider
on the ivory knob, engraved
after this photo was taken.
Not depicted is the sixth
and most dangerous predator of
all, the inventor of the weapon.
(Colt Arms reproduction of
the model 1852 revolver.)

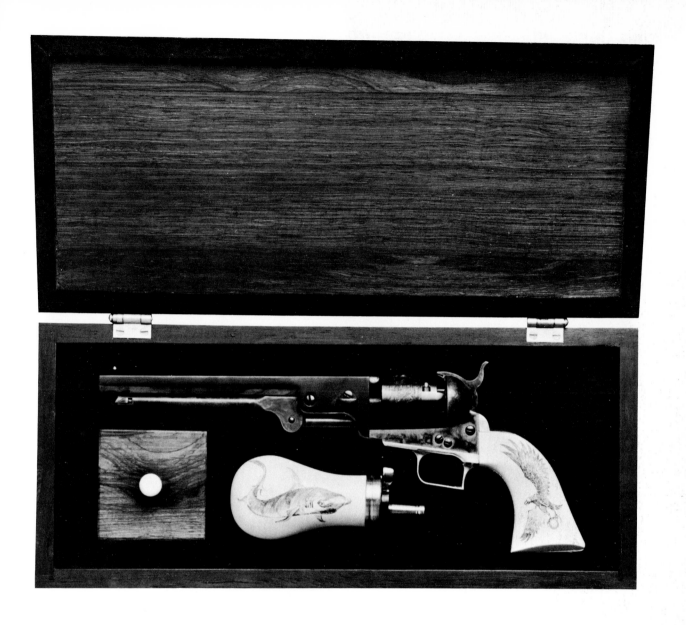

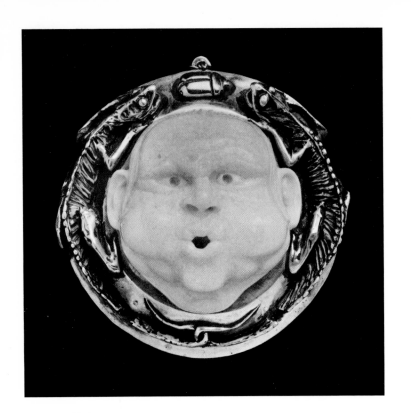
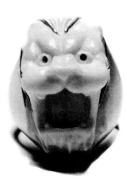
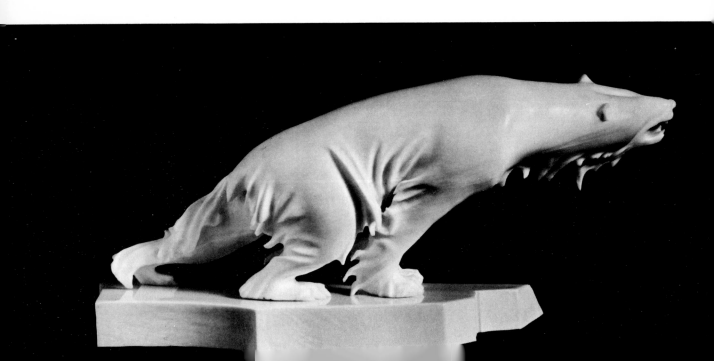

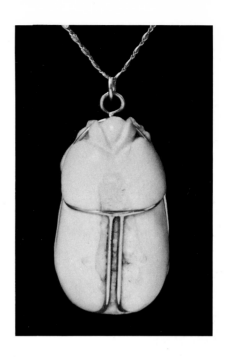

NORTH WIND *puffs from cast-silver pendant,*
far left, on which are two lizards, tails
entwined but severed, freeing them to bite
simultaneously the golden scarab at
the top. The Wind's head is carved from walrus
ivory, as is a roaring lion, near left, in
a ring with gold setting. Also of walrus is
the scarab, right, bound with gold, a
pendant. Below, two views of a polar bear,
carved from whale tooth (note the grain)
on an elephant ivory ice floe. This piece
was begun by an anonymous Norwegian artist,
finished by the author.

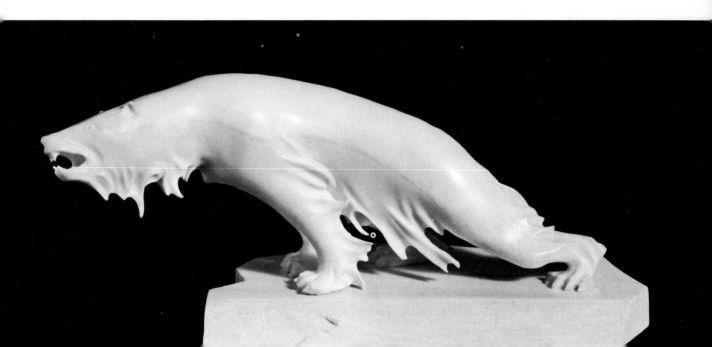

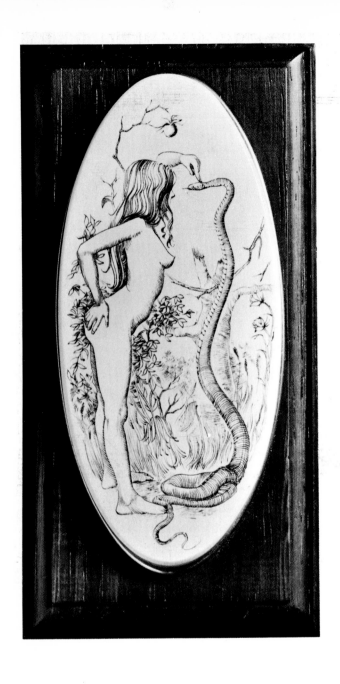

EVE converses with the serpent, left.
Over her head hangs the forbidden
fruit; engraving on an elephant ivory
plaque, framed with brass, mounted on
Brazilian rosewood base.

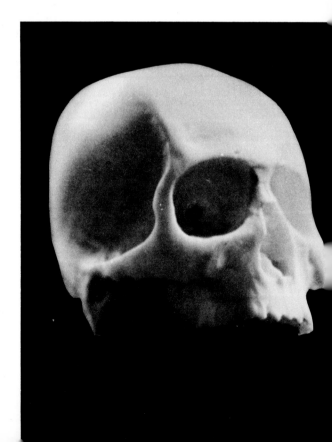

PORTRAIT head of woman, right, engraving on elephant ivory plaque in cocobolo wood base. Below, skull, symbol of the death-rebirth cycle, carved from a large whale tooth, mounted on a rosewood base.

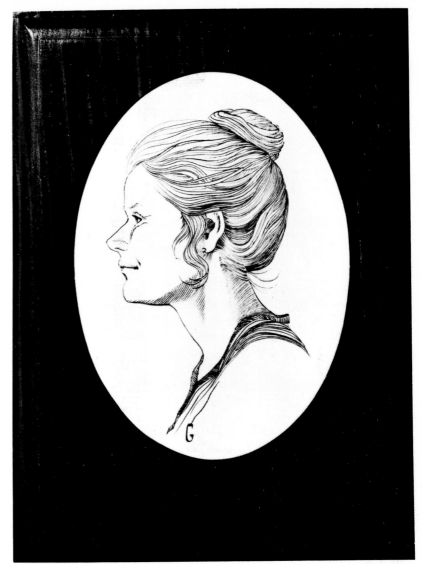

VII Fantasy and Imagery

DEATH BAGPIPES on an inverted whale tooth, shown here from three views, each displaying one of the piece's three figures. The bagpipe, in this case a zampogna from Italy, symbolizes all folly. Above is a profile view of the rosewood casket in which the piece rests.

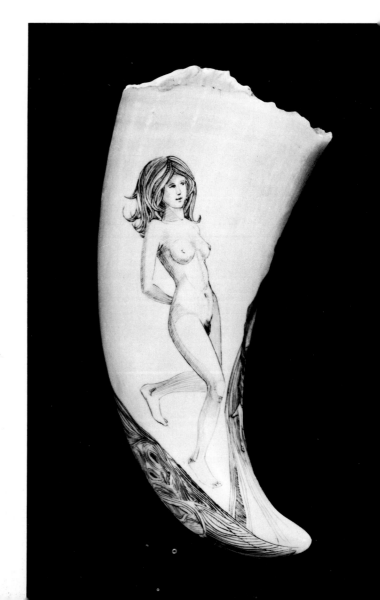

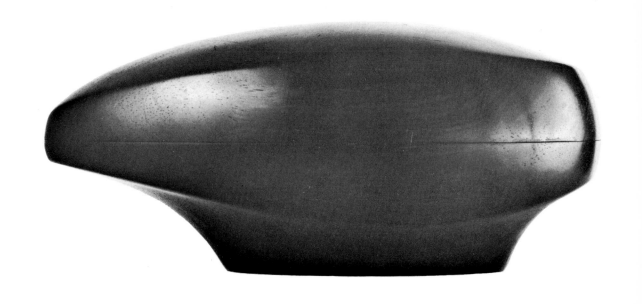

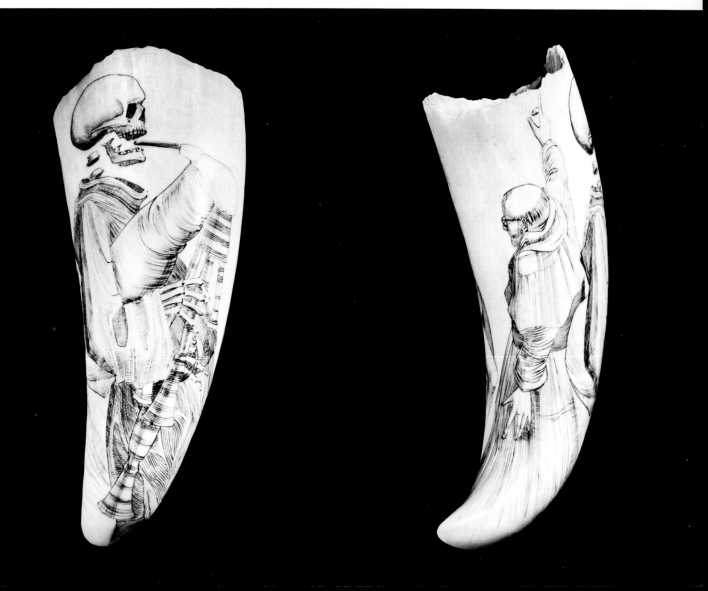

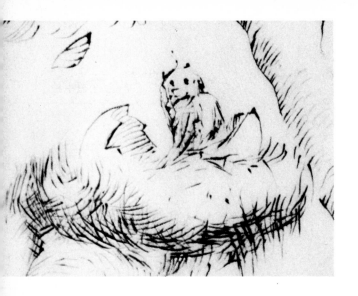

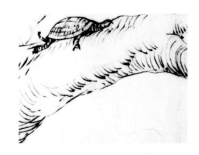

GNARLED tree
contains many secrets,
including peekers from
behind branches, a
rare spotted-tree
turtle, and someone who
has just hatched. A
hooded figure with a
staff is seated on a
limb, and appears to
be dangling a plum bob.

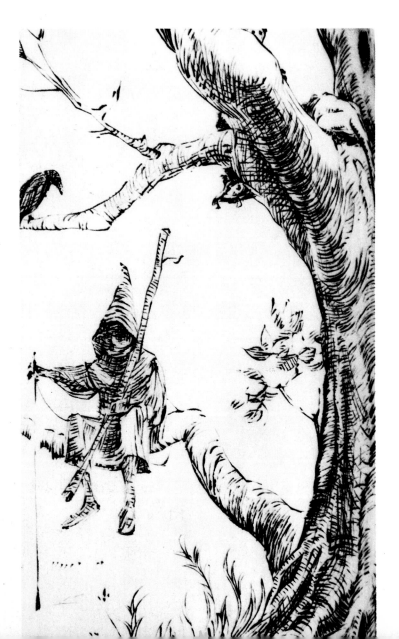

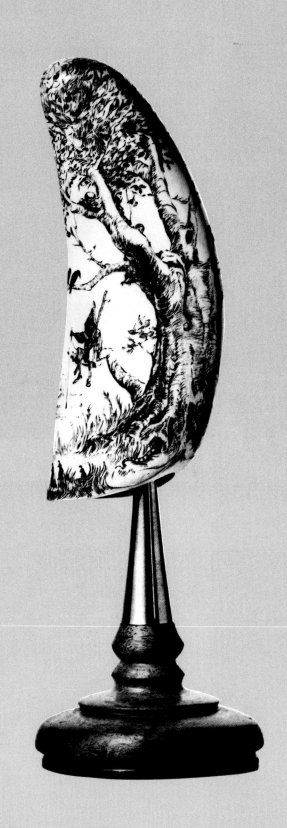

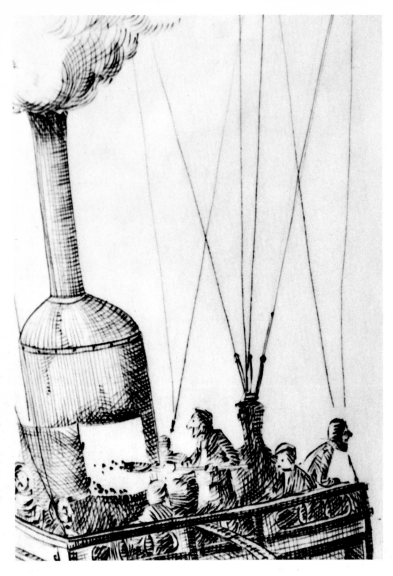

AEROSTATION by moonlight: huge balloons bearing heavy wooden wagons waft over a jagged landscape with mountains, pine trees and castle. Smoke, flames, and ash boil up from chimney of iron furnace as stoker shovels coals into the glowing fire. Passengers relax, sightsee.

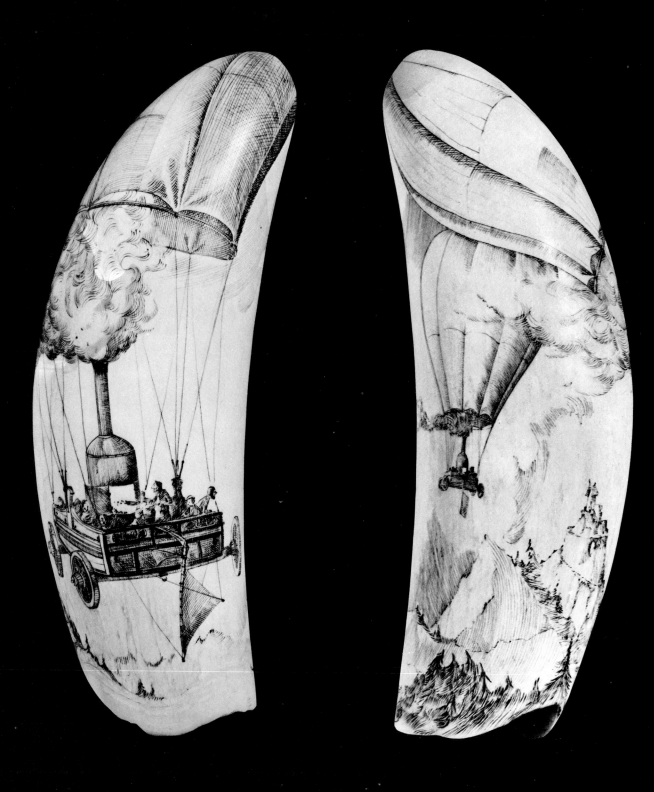

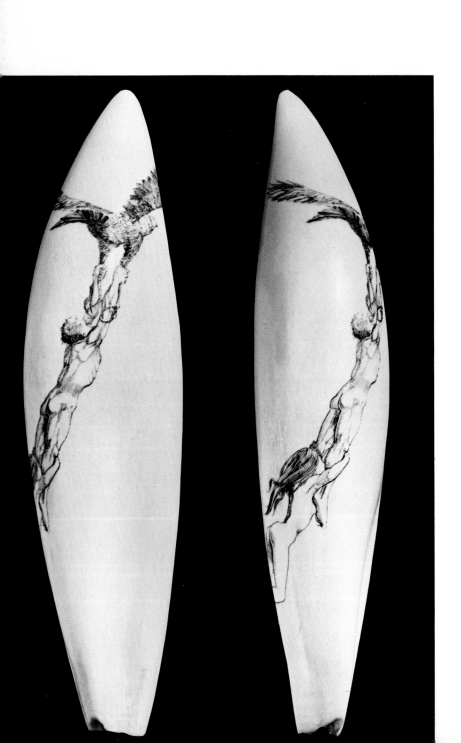
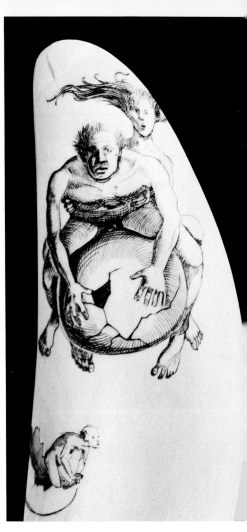

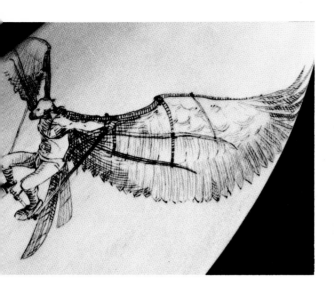

A TRIO of scrimshaw'd teeth,
right, makes a sculptural arrangement
atop tall brass spindles. The lowest
has jagged spines, a natural
deformity caused by calcification,
making the tooth point downward,
whence Icarus (face: not shown)
falls as Daedelus, above, hovers.
On the central piece in the set
people hurtle through space in level
flight, riding eggs which fracture,
opposite page, top. On the tallest
piece in the set, a man and woman
are lifted up by an eagle, two
views, opposite page bottom. The
base is rosewood, inlet with
elephant ivory with engraved
mariner's compass rose.

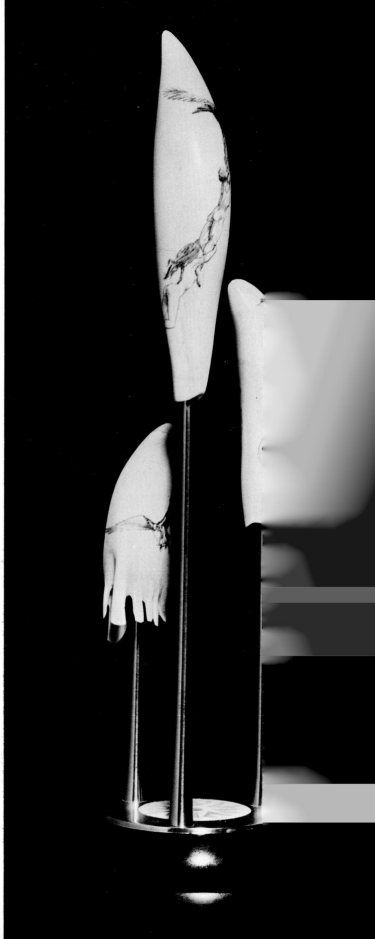

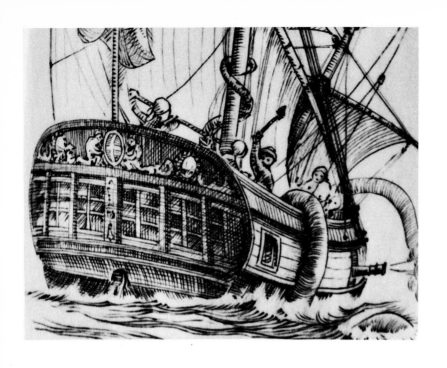

*VENTURESOME vessel with archaic rig
does battle with sea monsters: a
pair of scrimshaw'd whale teeth
on a rosewood stand. In the tooth at
the left, a giant squid-like creature
has thrown tentacles aboard the
vessel, one twirling around the mast;
crew chops away furiously with
axes, pikes. A cannon is fired at the
head of the intruder. Smoke billows.*

92

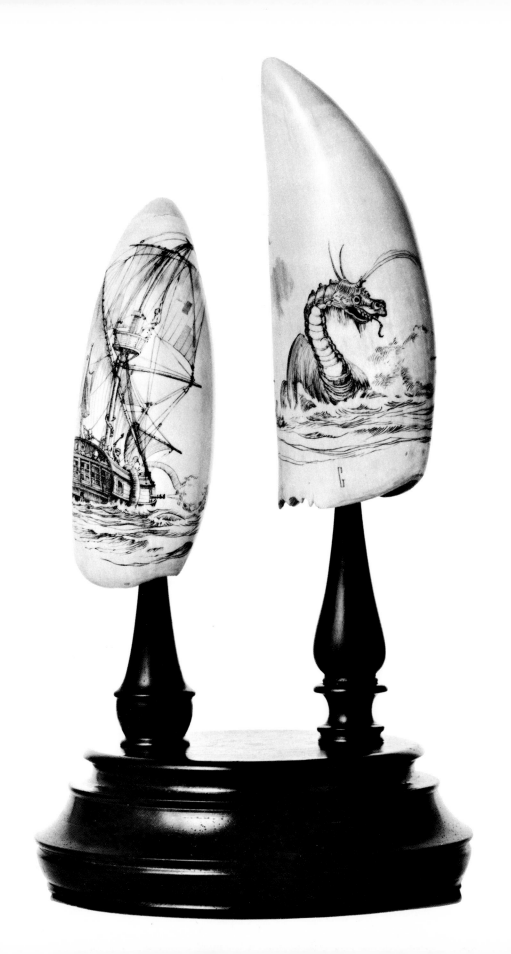

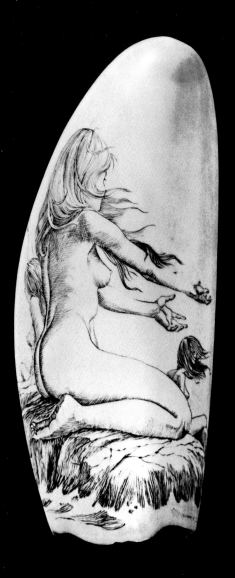
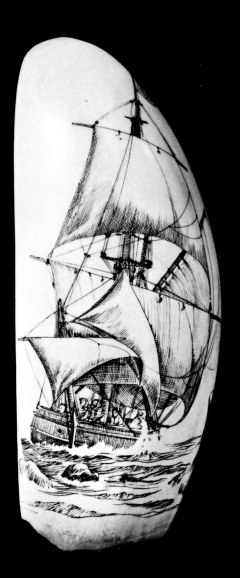
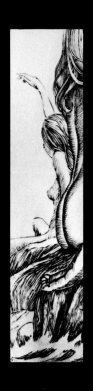

SIRENS SING, seductively beckoning a small ship toward disaster, above. Water churns around low dark rocks, barely visible from ship's deck, then the crew at last sees the danger and up goes the helm — too late, or in time?

On the opposite page, above, two views of a tiny boat thrashing into the wind, leeboards down, dolphins leaping before it, a volcano dimly visible on the horizon. Below, three views of another tooth, same boat, shown here running free, blown by Boreas. A lookout clings desperately to the masthead; ahead, a serpent rears up from the mysterious depths, menacing.

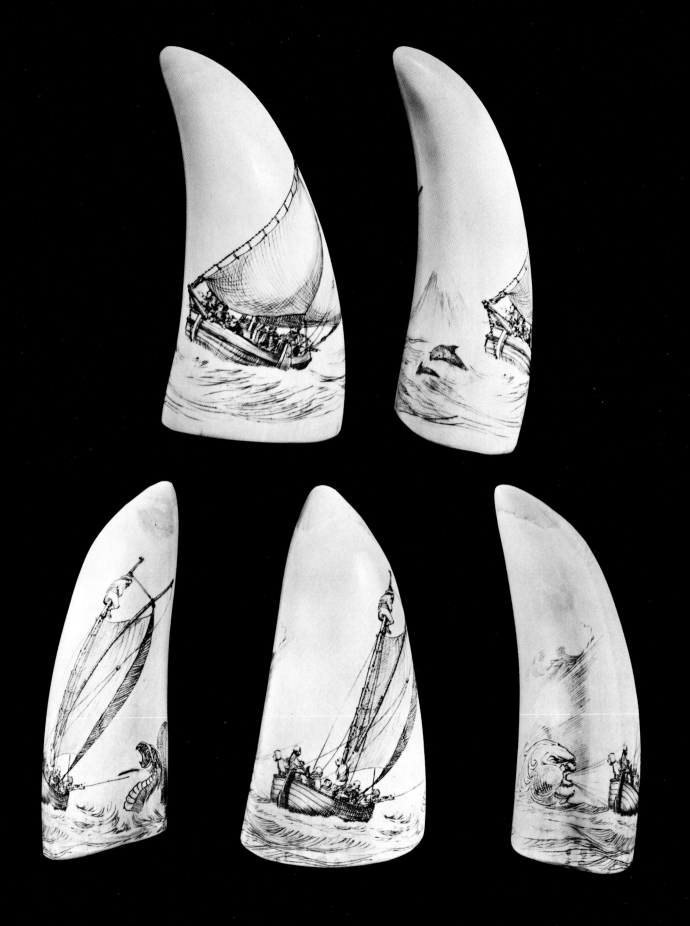

VIII Pirates

Even the average reader knows a good deal about pirates, no doubt having picked up the knowledge in childhood. Therefore it is only necessary here to summarize and make a composite picture of the average freebooter.

The pirate was swarthy, to begin with, and he was fond of garish raiment. His fingers, ears or nostrils were adorned with rings of gold or bone, he wore more personal armament and facial hair than either fashion or good taste dictated, he collected parrots and mynahs, he spat with great accuracy as a result of much practice, and bathing made him feel ever so much less the man.

Further, he picked his teeth with the tip of a cutlass, which was terribly hard on his gums, but helped terrify captives. These unfortunates frequently found him whimsical, seldom shared his sense of humor, and considered his silence preferable to his laughter.

Even so, he is a sympathetic figure, for although he collected loot from countless galleons and monasteries, he had to bury it somewhere amongst bones, with the result that, although well-off financially, he was denied access to his holdings by circumstances, and lived an underprivileged existence amongst colleagues who were without etiquette or culture.

The Pirate was given to knife throwing, gambling, arm wrestling, cards, and was, alas, all too frequently an ungracious loser. If one of his limbs ended in an iron hook or a wooden peg, he would be all the more dangerous at close quarters, but at a handicap if forced to chase an adversary into the rigging. And although he was cunning and treacherous when sober, his weakness for spirits was well known and frequently exploited by his foes.

He carried in his sock a yellowed and creased parchment, a map. It had cryptic markings and ominous dark stains. If he did *not* have a map, it was because it had been stolen from him by a shipmate as he lay insensate after a drunken debauch. He would then spend years tracking the thief,

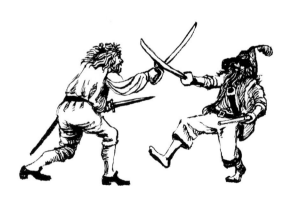

for the map was, of course, to his treasure, his only chance at social redemption, security, and the small inland farm which was his flickering dream.

Although poor at even simple arithmetic, he would be unerringly accurate at forecasting weather changes, as a result of his many old wounds which were barometrically active. The poor fellow's foul temper and ill manners become even more understandable when one considers the intolerable personal inconveniences which he was daily forced to endure as inherent to his profession: mites; toothache; oily, itchy scalp; sores; heartburn; athlete's foot; boils and insomnia.

When he did slumber, it was only lightly, and he was liable to awaken instantly at barely audible scraping sounds, rustlings or metallic clicks. His sleep was also hindered by nocturnal fevers, perspirations and tremblings induced by traumatic dreams, for which reason his eyes were always bloodshot. If a pirate mumbled things in his sleep, it was both pleasanter and safer not to listen.

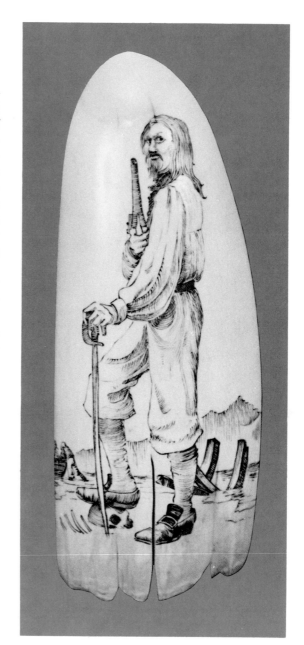

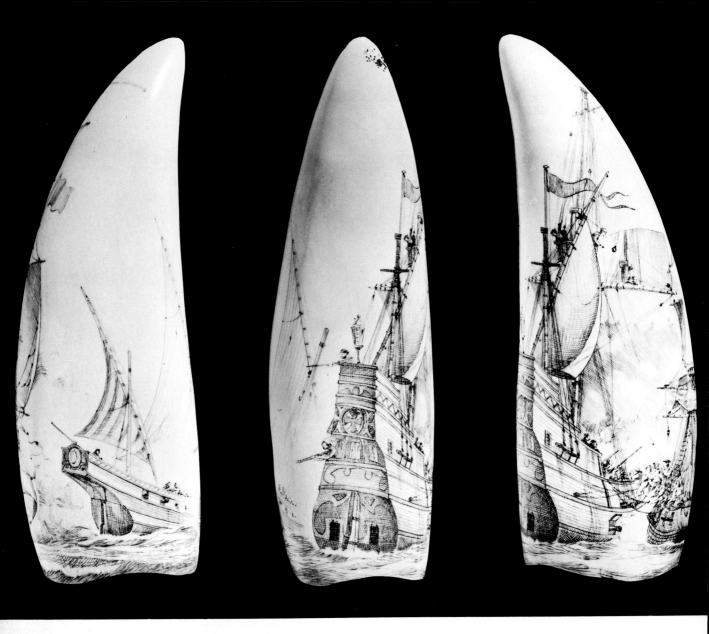

A LATEEN-RIGGED, fast piratical craft, left, is firing cannons and closing to windward of a large galleon. Boarding parties wait in readiness along her rails. The galleon, in the second view of this tooth, surges ahead under all sail. She is grappled to leeward by another pirate vessel from which boarders are swarming onto her (third view), although their small vessel is caught aback and being dragged stern first by the bigger ship (fourth view, far right). The action is at its crisis. Can the galleon's crew cut loose the grappling lines? If so, they will overwhelm the fierce but outnumbered boarders one by one, then deal with the other vessel separately, to return home with prisoners in chains, sullen and ominous but helpless. But if the lateener closes in time to join her cohort, together they will drive the hapless galleon's defenders below decks to be rounded up later, and dispatched or subjected to extraordinary indignities, or both. The chests of valuables will later be taken ashore to be buried amongst bones, and a map made of the locations.

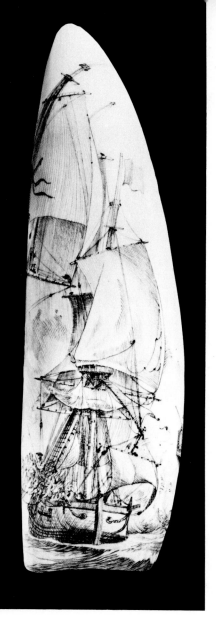

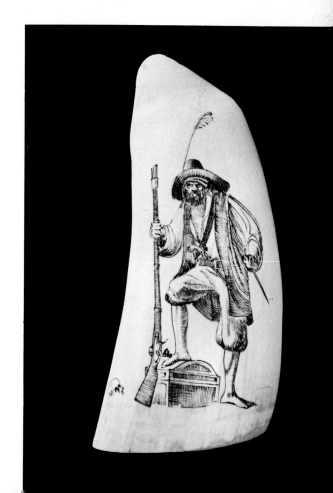

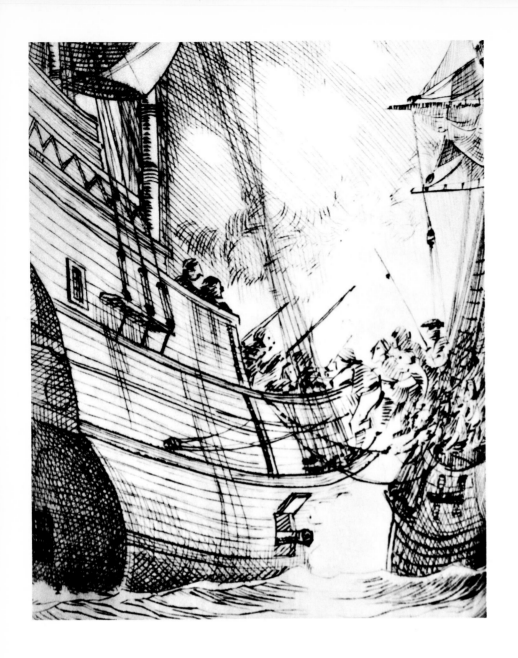

LONG JOHN SILVER is seated on his apple barrel, braced against the rolling of the ship, glancing sidelong at the world, scheming schemes and thinking of gold.

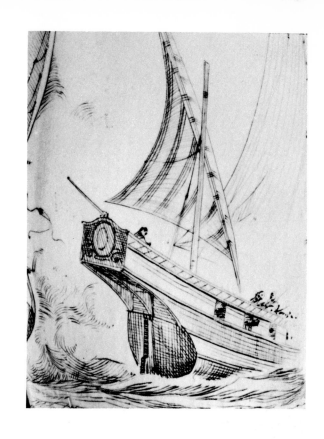

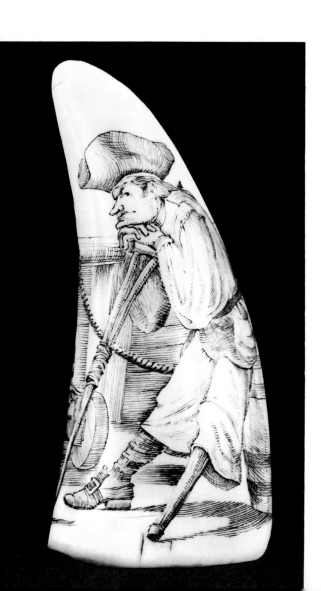

Most of the so-called buccaneers carried a document called a letter of marque, which was a written permission by a government to the captain of a privately-owned warship, or privateer, permitting him to capture the ships of enemy countries.

After an unrewarding, tedious voyage, it sometimes happened that a fat merchant vessel of a neutral country would come lumbering over the horizon, too much of a temptation to resist. Not too infrequently, a war would end before a privateersman was ready to quit, and so he would continue fighting it On His Own Account. In either case, he had technically become a pirate. But the label *Pirate* was widely used, and not always with technical accuracy.

One of the hardiest and most successful of the licensed freebooters was Woodes Rogers, an Englishman who in 1708 sailed with two ships, the *Duke* and *Duchess,* around Cape Horn into the Pacific ocean, there to nibble at Spain's farthest appendages of empire.

To the Spanish, Rogers was a pirate, though technically he was a privateer. He was an iron disciplinarian, much given to floggings, and very energetic. Within a short time in the Pacific he had captured several vessels and ransomed a couple of towns. In passing Juan Fernandez Island, he rescued an old buccaneer who had long been marooned there, one Alexander Selkirk, Daniel Defoe's Robinson Crusoe.

California was Roger's destination. Down this coast the fabulous treasure galleons passed, sailing from Manila for Acapulco with all the gold, gems, spices, and rich fabrics the Spaniards could wring from their East Indies empire to send back to Spain on the plump galleons, via Mexico.

Rogers placed his little squadron across the treasure route and waited. When a sail appeared, it was in fact one of the Manila ships. *Duke* and *Duchess* were cleared for action and their crews sent to quarters. From Roger's own record:

"I ordered a large kettle of chocolate to be made for our ship's company (having no spiritous liquor to give them), then we went to prayers, and before we had concluded were disturbed by the enemy firing at us. They had barrels hanging at each yardarm, that looked like powder barrels to deter us from boarding 'em."

Duke closed the stranger, exchanged several broadsides, then crossed her bows, raking her decks end to end with cannon fire. "So warmly that she soon struck her colours . . ."

She yielded some specie, 48,698 lbs. of silk, uncut gemstones, 7,200 "sattins flower'd with gold and silver," and 4,310 pairs of silk stockings. Two Englishmen

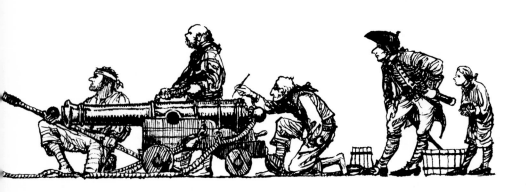

102

were wounded, one of them Rogers himself.

"I was shot through the left cheek, the bullet striking away a great part of my upper jaw and several of my teeth, part of which dropped down upon the deck." And later, "In the night I felt something clog my throat, which I swallowed with much pain, and suppose it's a part of my jawbone, or the shot which we can't yet give an account of." Thenceforth Rogers could not speak and issued his orders in writing. He is depicted thus, at the right, in a detail from a scrimshaw'd tooth.

Three days later, Christmas of 1709, a much bigger ship was sighted and attacked, but the newcomer, another Manila galleon, was so large and heavily built, the English cannon balls could not penetrate her. They, however, took a terrific mauling from her cannon fire before she sailed away unscathed, leaving Rogers worse off than ever: "... Part of my heel bone being struck out and all under my ankle cut above half through."

With all these wounds, unable to speak or walk, with damaged ships, off a hostile shore and without adequate medical aid, Rogers found the energy to quell a mutiny, refit his ships, reorganize his restless crews, cross the Pacific and return by way of the Cape of Good Hope to London where he was happily welcomed by all.

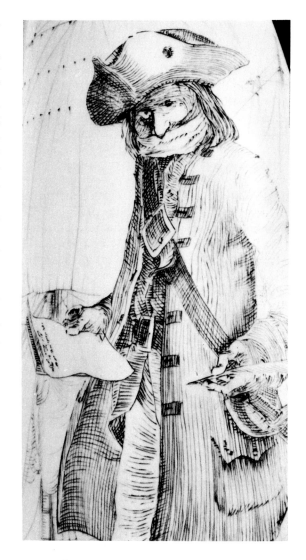

IX Tools and Techniques

It is said the scrimshaw tradition was a sailor amusing himself by carving or engraving. That is true of this scrimshander, although the circumstances are a couple of centuries different. The old sailors did the best they could to graphically depict subjects on whale teeth, and their work was naturally influenced by the styles of their time. The same is inescapably true of the scrimshanders of today. Conceptually, our approach is much the same as the old, but reflects our different conditioning.

Where the tools and techniques of scrimshaw are concerned, they also remain about the same today as always, but there are now more conveniences available. This last chapter will deal with some of these, and specifically with the approach of the author to the mechanics of ivory engraving.

Every whale tooth is different — unlike other forms of ivory where each tusk is much like the one before with only slight variations. Some whale teeth are long, curving and pointed, some are blunt and square, some cylindrical, rounded, and still others are slab-sided. The shape of the tooth will dictate the general design. If there is a specific purpose or design in mind, then a tooth must be selected of a shape that will complement it.

That is the case with the tooth which appears again and again in various phases of work on these pages. Shown in actual size, it was chosen for the purpose of presenting a step-by-step illustration.

The raw tooth is rough, with a grainy, furrowed surface, as in Figure 1, and must be polished smooth to be engraved. Ivory is easy to file, and may be cut down with a wood rasp and metal file to remove the deep pits and crevasses in the surface.

The same thing may be accomplished more quickly with an electrically powered drum sander, if the drum has a soft pad under the sandpaper. This is a very dangerous approach to the first step in polishing, however, because it may overheat the ivory. The friction of fast polishing will very quickly make the surface of the piece too hot, thereby changing it from soft to very brittle unless great care is taken. Hand filing, though slower, is far safer.

When the piece is completely filed down, a wide belt around its middle may be covered with black ink. This runs down into the deepest scratches and remains stubbornly in them until they are removed entirely with 120 grit sandpaper, the next (and slowest) phase of polishing (Figure 2). This must be done by hand. The upper and lower extremities of the tooth are avoided with the ink because those areas frequently contain hidden cracks or flaws which may be quite deep.

Once ink runs into such a crack, it is there forever, and its depth of penetration makes an ugly stain. It is important to carefully examine a piece of ivory for flaws before beginning work on it. The ink is used to expose the deep scratches which are very hard to see with the unaided eye.

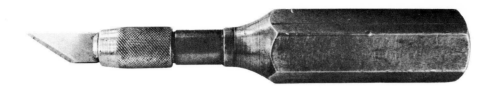

In this early stage the surface is as yet too rough to reflect the glare in which scratches are more visible.

When the piece is completely sanded with 120 grit, successive sandings with 180 grit and 220 grit will prepare the surface for the final step. Any kind of sandpaper will work, but best is white, opencoat silicon carbide sandpaper because it does not readily load up with ivory dust. This abrasive is available in nearly every chandlery.

Final polishing in this artist's system is a scrubbing with fine steel wool. This gives a satin surface to the ivory (as in Figure 3), which has just enough tooth to take pencil marks, but has a high enough polish to give a reflection. Many workers in ivory routinely prepare their work by buffing the piece to a high gloss. This is simple and seductive, for the surface of the ivory is nearly always destroyed by the process. Buffing almost inevitably overheats and makes it hard, brittle, and flinty, so an engraver's tool wants to skate across its surface rather than furrow through it. Buffing also renders the ivory unstable so that it frequently cracks. If a glossy finish is desired, let it be on ivory that is not to be engraved, and let it be applied with great care not to overheat the piece.

When the piece is prepared to take a design, the drawing may be done with a 2H or 3H pencil, a fine, hard lead that takes well on the ivory and can be sharpened to a needle point for a very thin line. The form of the piece will dictate the design, which may be entirely plotted in pencil. The steel wool makes a good eraser over broad areas; for erasing tiny details within larger areas that must stay, a sharpened eraser-pencil is very useful.

In Figure 4, the outline of San Francisco's museum ship *Balclutha*, once *Star of Alaska*, is taking form on the surface. The entire hull is drawn, even the underwater part which will later be lost. When the pencil design is applied, it is sprayed once or twice with artist's workable fixative. This is obtainable in art supply stores. It dries at once, after which the piece may be handled at will without the design being rubbed away.

When a complete outline is prepared in pencil, it is ready to be engraved. With what tool? Melville in *Moby Dick* tells us of Pequod's scrimshanders:

"Some of them have little boxes of dentistical-looking implements, especially intended for the scrimshandering business, but in general they toil with their jack knives alone."

This artist toils with his X-acto knife alone. It has a number 24 blade which is sharpened repeatedly as the work progresses. The blade is drawn across the ivory with a pulling motion, rather than pushing, as with the various chisel-pointed tools which gouge.

There is no correct tool for scrimshaw.

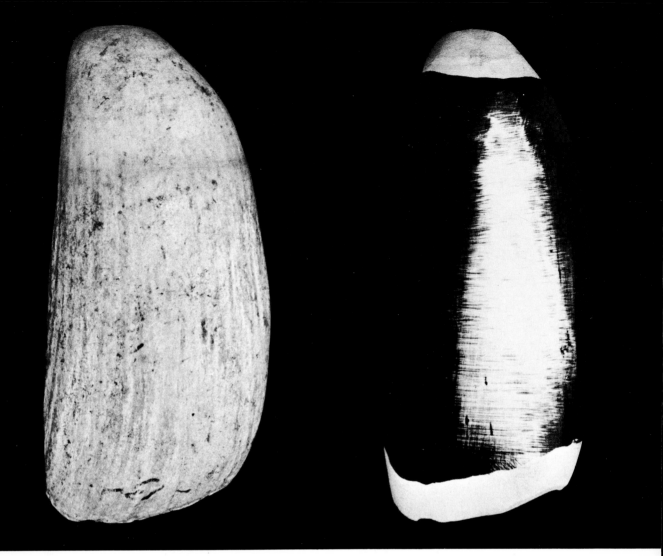

Figure 1   *Figure 2*

Each engraver works with the device that leaps easily into his hand. Bill Horgos (see page 28) uses a 78 rpm phonograph record needle held in a jeweler's pin vise; Rick Yager (see page 27) prefers an artist's push-pin embedded and taped into the end of a pen holder; Bob Spring (see pages 32-33) uses a small knife; Steve Wilson (see page 30) uses an orthodox engraver's tool. Others use sail or glovers' needles, scrivers, or re-ground scalpels.

The engraver was a tool repeatedly imitated by ancient sailors. They found that a small sail needle, with its fine steel and the same triangular cross-section as a standard engraver's tool, could have its tip broken off and then be sharpened and embedded in a cork or home-made handle for as good an engraver as could be desired by any professional.

Where the engraving itself is concerned, whatever lessons in style this book offers are recorded in the reproductions on the foregoing pages. If the reader has further questions on style, he is referred to Dürer, Schöngauer, Rembrandt, etc.

A strong direct light is important, a light which casts a reflection on the surface

106

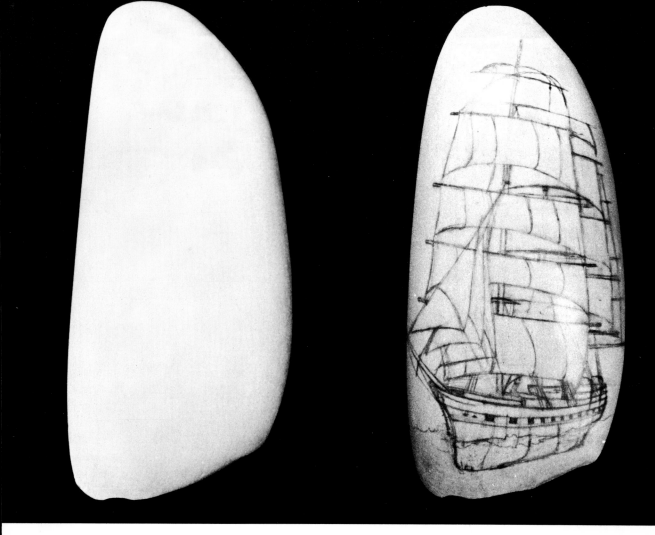

Figure 3

Figure 4

of the ivory. Only in a glare is it possible to see the line as it is cut. Alternatively, some artists (such as David Dubin, see page 31) coat the work with black so that the marks made by the tool show up white.

Magnification is very helpful, and can be obtained with any number of magnifying eyepieces with different powers and focal lengths, available from jeweler's supply houses. Some form of magnification is mandatory for really detailed work, and, in the long run, is much easier on the eyes.

In cutting the first outline, a light cut is usually the best, as it is easier to correct

if it wanders off course a bit. Sometimes it can be left as is, and another correcting line superimposed. Sometimes it is desirable to remove it, in which case the light line is much more easily shaved or rubbed out than a heavy one. An accurate first outline is very important. It is the skeleton to which the flesh of the completed work adheres.

A lightly cut line can frequently be erased by means of a very abrasive, grey-tipped typewriter eraser-pencil. Deeper lines must be shaved or filed out. Filing and repolishing is fastest but sometimes cannot

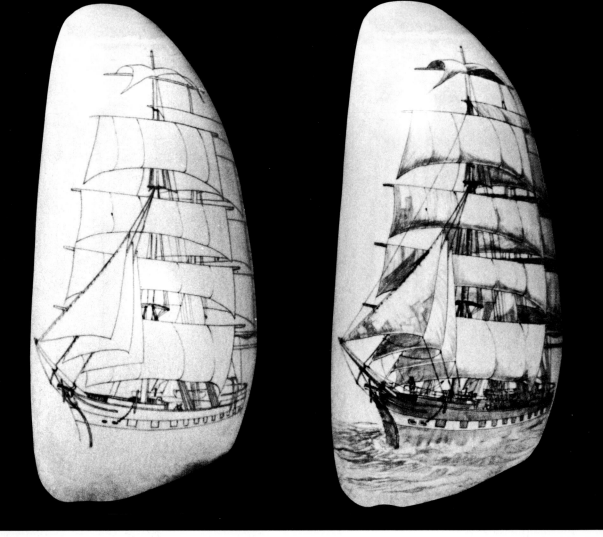

Figure 5   *Figure 6*

be used because the area to be removed is surrounded too closely by work that must remain. In that case it must be carefully shaved or scraped out with a sharp knife blade, then repolished with first a bit of light sandpaper wrapped around a match stick, then a little steel wool spun onto the end of the same stick. Also useful for this work are small, fine riffle files of the sort used by jewelers.

When the whole design has been etched, it is ready to be inked. India Ink is good. It may be applied with an old brush, then wiped or blotted away as much as

possible while still wet. Another application of steel wool will remove all the surplus ink, the dried coats of fixative and the pencil marks, leaving only the clean first engraving, as in Figure 5.

Other substances may be used to color the design: a wax crayon rubbed into the scratches, or various kinds of paint. A favorite of the old whalermen was lamp-black mixed with a bit of oil. The tooth pictured on the front and back covers of this book was done with Pelican colored inks which had been brought to a higher than normal intensity of pigmentation by means of evaporation. That is, the ink pots were intentionally left open for several days, until half their liquid was gone, leaving a denser substance in the bottles.

After a satisfactory outline is inked and ready, it may be filled in with pencil marks indicating the next areas to be engraved. Figure 6 shows *Balclutha* in this stage. The work has its tones and values, its lights and darks, planned out. The guidelines are there for the closely controlled line patterns to follow.

This is the stage where it is easy to let the mind wander from the work. As the hand cuts the endless series of parallel strokes, it is tempting to allow the movements to become mechanical. If this happens, the finished work has a mechanical and sterile look to it. The only way to avoid this is to love each stroke of the tool, each line, no matter how unimportant seeming within the whole framework. Any tendency to rush a tedious area must be avoided, and that area given as much attention as if it were the soul of the whole work. The tedious areas demand great patience; they create the space in which the highlights live.

There is no particular limit to the number of inkings which can be applied to a piece. Very complicated works may take dozens and dozens. If steel wool is used to polish repeated inkings, it will begin to wear down the existing design. This effect can be used intentionally for heightened contrasts, by permitting some lines to lighten, while others are darkened by re-cutting.

The finished *Balclutha* is illustrated in Figure 7, and again in greatly magnified detail in Figure 9. The reverse face of the piece is shown in Figure 8, a small profile view of the same vessel under shortened sail. Also illustrated is the display stand, a rosewood base with turned brass spindle.

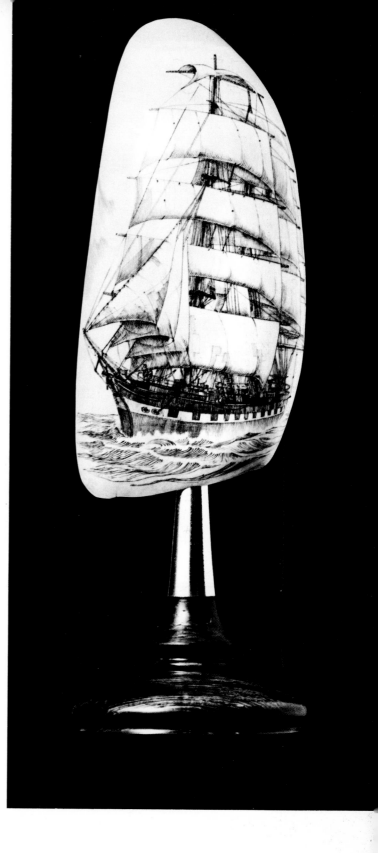

Figure 7

109

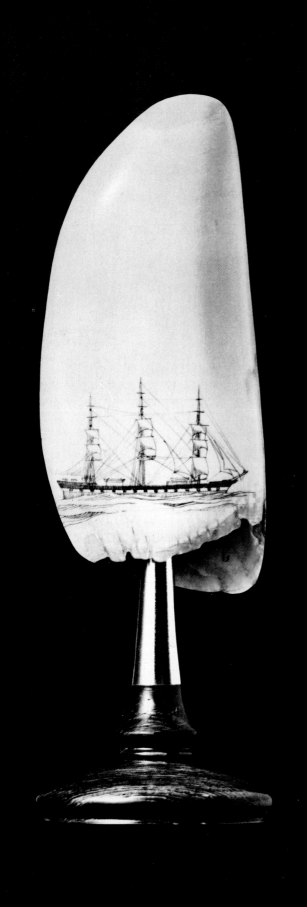

The cavity of the tooth was drilled out to a slight depth to accomodate the spindle tip. The tooth turns freely and can be lifted off the stand for handling.

The manner in which finished work is displayed depends on the type of piece, how it has been worked and designed. The spindle is good for a vertical piece; for a horizontal work, a plaque or casket may look best.

Ivory is very tough stuff in most ways, but again it is vulnerable to heat. When worked with a power tool, it must not be allowed to become warm to the touch. Often it will crack after being overheated, even in the midst of being worked. Another thing that will cause a piece in progress to crack is being held too long and too close under a bright, hot, light bulb. For this reason, small high-intensity lamps are safest, though a hotter bulb can be used if the piece is not held too close.

Ivory will crack if exposed to direct sunlight, and should not be left on windowsills. Another circumstance which will cause checking or cracking is moving a piece of ivory from a humid to an arid climate. Ivory wants to be kept cool and damp. Merchants in San Francisco's Chinatown keep ivory statuary behind glass with cups of water in the cases to increase the already high humidity.

If ivory is being kept in a warm, dry environment, it must be wrapped in wet towels or rags, and white ones at that. Colored dyes can drive into the surface of the ivory. Many substances are ivory dyes. Even wet sawdust stains ivory.

When a work in progress does develop cracks, they must be attended to at once, for even a small amount of ink running into one will create an indelible, ugly stain and possibly destroy the piece. If a crack is fine, not gaping, a design can sometimes

Figure 8

still be worked across without its taking the ink if the crack is heavily sprayed with layers of fixative to fill and cover. This may be applied very thickly, for it does not impede the knife and will ultimately be removed.

If a crack opens wide, it must be more solidly filled. Epoxy mixed with ivory powder solves the problem. Although the repaired crack remains visible, it is sealed and can be worked over with the tool. Epoxy can be engraved when hardened, although it is considerably softer than the surrounding ivory surface. It is important that epoxy be mixed thoroughly and in correct parts. This can best be done on glass with a palette knife, mixing in as much ivory powder (filings) as seems desirable. Whole broken areas of a piece can be built up and restored with this substance, then filed and polished flush.

Besides whale, there are five other main types of ivory: elephant, walrus, hippopotamus, narwhal and boar. The last three are seldom used for engraving. Hippo ivory is not readily available and is extremely hard. In fact it is the hardest of all ivories, bluish and flinty when freshly cut. It can be engraved but works more like metal and quickly dulls tools. Even a big hippo tusk is not big enough to cut into sizable pieces.

Narwhal ivory is from the spiralled, tapering spear which grows from the forehead of the narwhal, a small arctic whale seldom taken. His spear, once thought to be from the unicorn, may reach eight feet in length and some three inches in diameter at the base. It is very rare and is seldom cut, for it has considerable beauty and value unadorned.

Boar's tusks are small and yield less volume of ivory than any of the other kinds. Elephant ivory is soft, easily scribed,

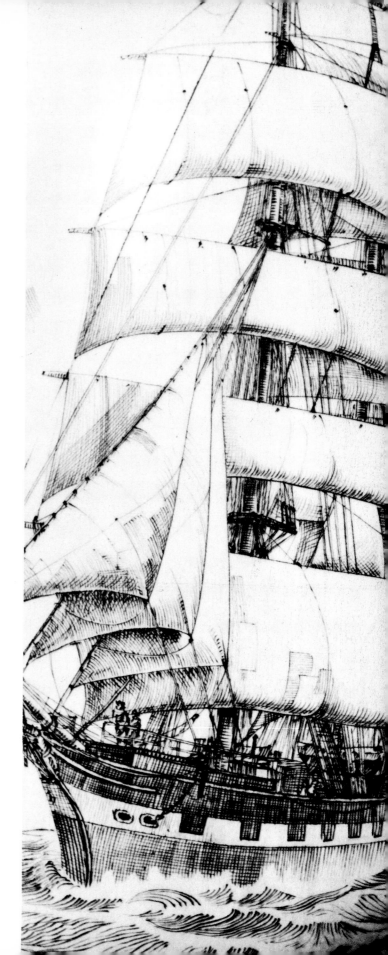

Figure 9

has a pleasing grain which forms criss-cross patterns when it is cut crosswise.

African elephants are currently being killed in unprecedented numbers for their tusks by poachers raiding ill-guarded game preserves. The depredations of these men are so reducing herds, they threaten to force elephant ivory up in value until there are no more elephants. At the time of this writing none of the elephant families are yet listed on the endangered species list.

The same is true of the walrus, whose ivory has been used for carving by Western man since before Christ, and in more recent times for engraving. Etched walrus ivory is not cut, for under the enamel layer the inner pulp is exceptionally porous, filled with tiny pits and flaws that will uncontrollably absorb the ink in accidental and unsightly patterns. This inner meat adapts itself to carving, and may even be used to intentionally contrast with the more dense outer material.

For instance, on page 80 is a wind face carved from walrus ivory. Its texture gives the distorted countenance an apoplectic look, as though thousands of blood vessels are bursting with the effort of the massive puff.

Frequently asked questions about scrimshaw pertain to the durability of the medium:

"Can it be handled? What effect does the oil and moisture from hands have on ivory?"

"What happens if you drop a whale tooth?"

"What happens if it gets wet?"

"Does the ink stay in the cracks forever?"

Scrimshaw not only can be handled, it *should* be for the art has a tactile aspect, as mentioned. Skin oil may or may not cause slight variances in patina.

Ivory is tough and will not shatter if dropped unless it has been made extraordinarily brittle by boiling. Whale teeth were frequently removed from the jaw by a boiling process which was less laborious than cutting them out. However the latter method left the ivory soft, the former did not.

Ivory is easily scratched, and it should be handled carefully. A fall on concrete might not break a whale tooth, but it would seriously damage its surface.

The various inks used in scrimshaw generally remain stubbornly in the cuts. Some pieces two centuries old remain in excellent condition, and others which have suffered obvious abuse have come through in relatively good shape.

In San Francisco, an elderly couple recently read about scrimshaw and realized that the curious object which had served as a doorstop in their kitchen for years was an immense whale tooth covered with engraving. Although it had been much kicked, the design was clear and sharp, except in the flat bald spot worn in the middle of one side, where it had slid around on the floor.

Scrimshaw is unquestionably one of the most durable art forms, but it is not totally impervious to a determined assault. Recently a lady found a large, handsome scrimshaw'd whale tooth amongst the dust and cobwebs of her attic. It was a wondrous thing, but too yellow and dirty for presentation, so she cleaned it up — with hot water, cleanser, scouring pads and good old elbow grease.

She removed dirt, patina, ink, and most of the surface — everything but an occasional wistful ghost of the original design, a fully rigged ship, dimly visible only under a strong light, sailing in a fogbank from which she will never emerge.

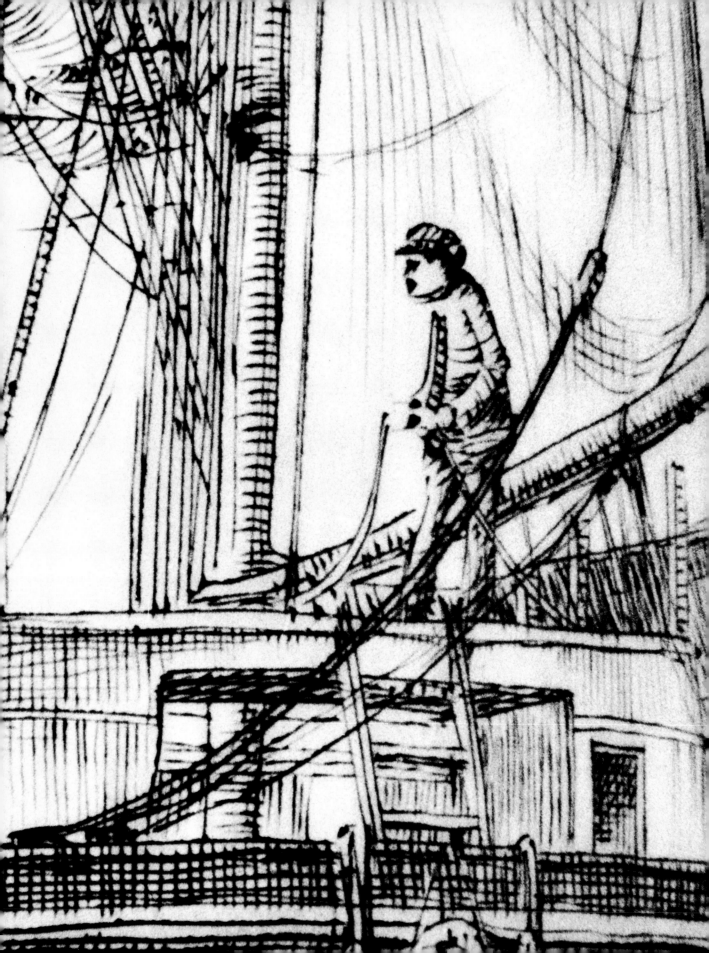

Acknowledgements

Of those people who have assisted with the preparation of this book, or the work illustrated in it, the author is particularly grateful to:

The entire staff of the San Francisco Maritime Museum, especially to Karl Kortum, Director, for his Introduction, and for endless information, assistance and encouragement; to Sarah Nome behind her towering stacks of paper, and to Matilda Dring behind her somewhat smaller piles of photos; each in her own way always managing to produce just the thing needed; to Danee McFarr for incidentals large and small; to Curator Harlan Soeten for commentary and criticism; to David Hull for his toil amongst all those books; to Charles Porter, below, in the labyrinth, and to Mrs. Walton, guardian of the ship.

To those cheerful master photographers, Dean Stone and Hugo Steccati of San Francisco for the photo portrayal of the vast majority of the pieces illustrated in these pages; where not otherwise credited, the photography of the author's work is theirs, and this book is as much a testimonial to their expertise as to the scrimshaw they have portrayed.

To Ward Dunham for the first whale tooth; to Nicholas Sidjakov for general guidance and specific help with this volume's design; to Bea Ferrigno, also for design help and for preparing these pages for the printer; to fellow craftsmen Ed Stiles, Arrigo D'Albert and Oliver Seeler for their assistance with some of the crafted pieces in Chapters VI and VII, and to Harriet Keith, secretarial pool of one.

To colleagues John Stobart, Howie Rosenfeld and Rick Yager for companionship, humor and commentary; to Norman Flayderman, Douglass C. Fonda, Jr., M. V. Brewington and Richard C. Kugler for technical and material assistance; to Ulf Gummeson for his hospitality during my research in Massachusetts; to Jackson, polisher of many whale teeth, for keeping the shop fires going while this work went forward, and most of all to his mother, Kerstin, air spirit of Troll Hall, for her patience, warmth and helpfulness beyond measure. To her this work is dedicated.

Thanks also go to the people and institutions who have permitted pieces of my work in their ownership to be reproduced here:

Ed Ross, for *Gay Head* and *Lettitia* in the ice, pages 42 and 43, and the whaling pair, page 50; The San Francisco Maritime Museum, San Francisco, California, for the whaling set, pages 44 through 47, and for *California's* bones, page 51; Kjeld Jensen, *Charles W. Morgan,* pages 48 and 49; Dr. Norman C. Bunker, H.M.S. *Victory,* pages 52 through 55; Tom Kaye, sloop *Ferrett,* page 57; The International Marine Manuscript Archives, Inc., Nantucket, Mass. for U.S.F. *Constitution,* page 58; William Burger, U.S.F. *Constitution* set, pages 59 through 61; The United States Naval Institute, Annapolis, Maryland, for *BonHomme Richard,* page 63; Donald Osenkop, catboat *Andy,* page 64, yawl *Dandy,* page 72, Long John Silver, page 101; Jill Titus, Elephant ivory plaque with Eve and serpent, page 82; Jackson Gierhart, scow schooner *Alma,* page 64; Norman de Vall, ketch *Fri,* page 65; Ulf Gummeson, *Regalskeppet Wasa,* page 65; Dr.

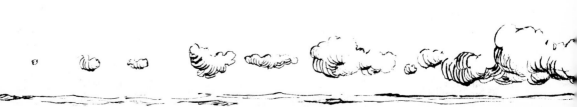

Duane Busch, M/Y *Seaplay,* page 66; Scott Newhall, Tyne tug *Eppleton Hall,* page 67; Roy Pasqualetti, Jr., model steam launch *Belle,* page 67; Karl Kortum, ketch *Griffyn,* page 71; Dr. Wylie H. Mullen, Jr., Colt Navy revolver set, pages 78 and 79; Ture Helleberg, polar bear, pages 80 and 81; Kerstin Gierhart, scarab pendant, page 81, and little boat blown by Boreas, page 95; Chogyam Trungpa Rinpoche, ivory skull, page 82; Heather Peterson, north wind pendant, page 80; Anna Helleberg, portrait plaque, page 83; Siegfried Reinhardt, death piping, pages 84 and 85; Judith Creasy, secret tree, pages 86 and 87; George D. Lawrence, fantasy with balloons, pages 88 and 89, also Woodes Rogers tooth, detail on page 103; Calvin Malone, ship vs. monsters pair, pages 92 and 93; Malcolm Whyte, sirens, page 94; Rich Wasserman, little boat with dolphins, page 95; Leonard Sarnat, pirate, page 97; George Schneider, pirate, page 99; Dean Stone, *Balclutha,* pages 106 through 111; David Dubin, whaleboat, page 116; Harold Sommer, schooner *Wanderbird,* page 118; Danee McFarr, tiny vessel and crew of one, the final illustration.

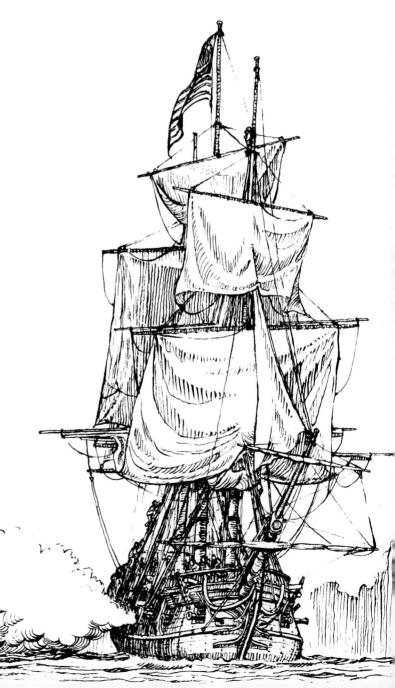

Bibliography

This bibliography is condensed and in two sections. The first lists major references on scrimshaw and whaling. Scholars interested in pursuing historical scrimshaw in greater depth should begin with Norm Flayderman's work listed below; it is the most definitive comment on the antique aspects of the subject to date. Anyone whose special interest is whaling rather than scrimshaw should begin by reading Melville's Moby Dick.

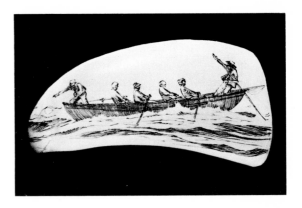

Ashley, Clifford W., *The Yankee Whaler,* Boston: Houghton Mifflin Co. Inc., 1938

Barbeau, Marius, "All Hands Aboard Scrimshawing," *The American Neptune,* Vol. XII, No. 2; Peabody Museum of Salem, 1966.

Barnes, Clare, Jr., *John F. Kennedy, Scrimshaw Collector,* Boston; Little, Brown and Co., 1969.

Bullen, Frank T., *The Cruise of the Cachalot,* New York: International Book and Publishing Co., 1899.

Burrows, Fredrika Alexander, *The Yankee Scrimshanders,* Taunton: William S. Sullwold Publishing Co., 1973.

Church, Albert Cook, *Whale Ships and Whaling,* New York: W. W. Norton and Co., 1938.

Flayderman, E. Norman, *Scrimshaw and Scrimshanders, Whales and Whalemen,* New Milford: N. Flayderman and Co., Inc., 1972.

Forbes, Allan, Jr., *The Story of Whaling,* Catalogue to Allan Forbes Whaling Collection Exhibit, Nantucket: Nantucket Historical Association, 1961.

Melville, Herman, *Moby Dick,* New York: Harper and Brothers, 1851.

Scammon, Charles M., *The Marine Mammals of the North-Western Coast of North America together with an account of the American Whale Fishery,* San Francisco: John H. Carmany, 1874.

Shapiro, Irwin, *The Story of Yankee Whaling,* New York: American Heritage Publishing Co., Inc., New York, 1959.

Stackpole, Edouard A., *Scrimshaw at Mystic Seaport,* Mystic: The Marine Historical Association, Inc., 1958.

The remainder of the list contains primarily pictorial books, offered for their graphic reference value to a scrimshander; each in its own way offers some special visual feeling of the reality of wooden sailing ships.

Brewington, M. V. and Dorothy, *Marine Paintings and Drawings in the Peabody Museum,* Salem: Peabody Museum, 1968.

Casson, Lionel, *Illustrated History of Ships and Boats,* New York: Doubleday and Co., Inc., 1964.

Chapman, Henry Friderico, *Architectura Navalis Mercatoria,* Stockholm, 1768 (reprinted by Praeger Publishers, New York, 1971).

Horgan, Thomas P., *Old Ironsides,* Boston: Burdette and Co., Inc., 1963.

Landström, Björn, *The Ship,* New York: Doubleday and Co., Inc., 1961.

Lever, Darcy, *A Young Sea Officer's Sheet Anchor or a Key to the Leading of Rigging and to Practical Seamanship,* London: 1818 (reprinted by Edward W. Sweetman Co., New York, 1963).

Longridge, C. Nepean, *The Anatomy of Nelson's Ships,* Hemel Hempstead, Hertfordshire, England: Model and Allied Publications, Ltd., 1961.

MacGregor, David R., *Fast Sailing Ships, 1775-1875,* Switzerland: Edita Lausanne, 1973.

Peabody Museum, "Photographs of Whaling Vessels," *The American Neptune,* Pictorial Supplement XV, Salem: Peabody Museum, 1973.

Rogers, Cedric, *Sailing Ships,* New York: Western Publishing Co., Inc., 1974.

Svensson, Sam, *Sails Through the Centuries,* New York: The Macmillan Company, 1962.

Villiers, Alan, *Men, Ships, and the Sea,* Washington, D.C.: National Geographic Society, 1962.

Absent in the above list are the books of Howard Chapelle, certainly America's dean of marine historians. His works are not primarily picture books, but their combined collections of drafts and plans of hundreds of American vessels, big and small, are invaluable to any illustrator seeking accuracy in the portraiture of these or vessels of their type.

Index

Allan Forbes Whaling Collection, 8, 9
Alliance, the, 59, 63
Alma, the, 56, 64
Anderson, Capt. Lloyd, 29
Andy, the, 64
Artifacts, crafted, 8, 10, 12, 16, 35
Ashley, Clifford, 8, 12, 15
    quoted, 8, 15
Aurora, the, 21

Balclutha, the, 56
    on scrimshaw, 105, 107, 108, 109, 110, 111
Baleen, defined, 9
Baskerville, Geoffrey, 3
Basques as early whalers, 8, 9
Belle, the, on scrimshaw, 67
Benjamin Cummings, the, log of, quoted, 12
Boar's tusks, 111
BonHomme Richard, the, 59, 61, 63
    on scrimshaw, 6, 62, 63
Brewington, M.V., 9
Bullen, Frank T., quoted, 51

Cahill, Tom, 28
California, the, 51
California, whaling out of, 16, 17, 20-21, 46
California gray whale, 46-47
Chapelle, Howard, 59
Charity, the, 34
Charles Phelps, the, 10
Charles W. Morgan, the, 17, 23, 48, 49, 56
Cold Spring Harbor Whaling Museum, 3
Colt Navy revolver and accessories, scrimshaw'd, 78-79
Constitution, U.S.F., 56, 58, 59
    on scrimshaw, 60, 71
Corset busks, 10, 13
Cracks, ivory, 110-11
Cruise of the Cachalot, 51
Curley, Capt. James, 28
Cutlass, the, on scrimshaw, 68, 71, 73
Cyane, H.M.F., on scrimshaw, 60

Dandy, the, on scrimshaw
Delano, Milton, 24
Down to the Sea in Ships (film), 49
Drawing, design, techniques of, 105
Dubin, David, 31, 107
Duchess, the, 102
Duke, the, 102

Ear bones, sperm whale, 25-26
Earle, Walter, quoted, 3
Elephant ivory, 111-12
Endangered species
    elephant as, 112
    whale as, 36-39 (*see also* Legislation, restrictive)

Endangered Species Act of 1973, The, 37
    (*see also* Legislation, restrictive)
Engraving, *See* Scrimshaw, new; Scrimshaw, old, engraved; Techniques: Tools, engraving
Eppleton Hall, the, on scrimshaw, 67, 70
Eskimos, scrimshaw of, 17

Ferrett, the, 56, 59
    on scrimshaw, 57
Flayderman, Norman, 5, 8, 13, 29-30
    quoted, 8, 30
Fletcher, Eric, 34
Fletcher, Marianne, 29
Fonda, Douglass C., Jr., 23
Fri, the, 65
Friendship sloop, 73

Galloway, Lyle, 33
Gam, last, 20-21
    on scrimshaw, 30
Gay Head, the, 20-21, 70
    on scrimshaw, 30, 42-43
Greenwich Maritime Museum, 56, 61
Griffyn, the, 2, 34
    on scrimshaw, 70, 71
Guerriere, H.M.F., on scrimshaw, 60

Hall, Gurdon, journal of, quoted, 10, 13
Hippo ivory, 111
Holland, early scrimshaw from, 9
Horgos, William, 28, 106
Hull, C.R., 30
Hussey, Capt. Christopher, 9

Ink, use of in scrimshaw, 104, 108-109
International Marine Manuscript Archives, Inc., 58
Ionides, Cyril, quoted, 2
Ivory
    care of finished, 112
    care of, in working, 110-11
    kinds of, 111-12

Jacobs, A. Douglas, 28
Jagging wheel, 10, 11
Japan, whaling in, 37
Java, H.M.F., on scrimshaw, 60
John and Winthrop, the, 21
John Bunyan, the log of, quoted, 6
Johnson, Melvin, 31
Jones, John Paul, 6, 55, 59, 61, 63

Kalliope, the, 2, 71
Kendall Whaling Museum, 7, 9, 12, 13, 17, 28
Kennedy, John F., 19, 24
Keppel, Admiral, 55
Kortum, Karl, 2-3, 20

Legislation, restrictive
    effect of, on scrimshaw, 19-20, 27-28, 38-39
    effect of, on whaling, 37

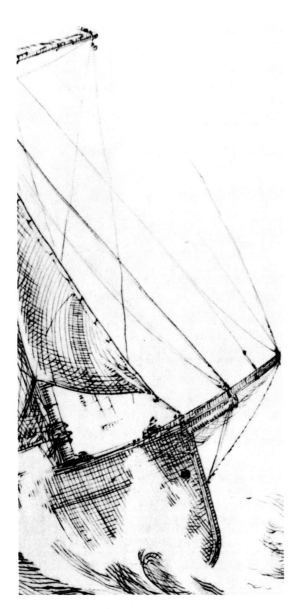

NORTH SEA schooner Wanderbird *leaps from a sea, blown by a storm and triple-reefed. This detail is from a tooth scrimshaw'd by the author, aboard the vessel.* Wanderbird *was launched in 1874 and is undergoing restoration in Sausalito, California.*

Endangered Species Act of 1973, The, 37
Lettitia, the, 20-21, 70
   on scrimshaw, 30, 42-43
Levant, H.M. War Sloop, on scrimshaw, 60, 61
Light, importance of, in engraving, 18, 106-107
Line plans, scrimshaw done from, 56, 59
Long John Silver, on scrimshaw, 100

Macomber, "Sperm Whale Jimmy," 20-21
Marine Mammals of the Northwestern Coast, 47
Masefield, John, quoted, 53
Melville, Herman, 8, 16, 105
   quoted, 16, 105
Myrick, Frederick, 18, 19
Mystic Seaport, Conn., 17, 49

Nantucket, Mass., whaling out of, 8, 9-10
Nantucket Whaling Museum, 23
Narwhal ivory, 111
New Bedford, Mass., 5, 22, 23, 48
New Bedford Whaling Museum, 11, 16, 23
Newhall, Scott, 66, 67
Nile, the, 10

Oakland, Calif., 21, 51
Oakland Museum, 29
Pan bone, sperm whale, 33
Perry, William, 22-24
Pirates, 96-103
Polishing, final, techniques of, 105
Princess Royal, the, 61, 63
Prisoners, scrimshaw by, 17

Rogers, Woodes, quoted, 102-103
Rosenfeld, Howie, 31
Russia, whaling in, 37

Sanding, techniques of, 104-105
San Francisco, whaling out of, 16, 17, 20-21
San Francisco Maritime Museum, 2-3, 4, 6, 14, 15,
   20, 21, 47, 66
Scammon, Charles M., 46-47
Scrimshanders, new
   advantages enjoyed by, 35
   Anderson, Capt. Lloyd, 29
   Delano, Milton, 24
   Dubin, David, 31, 107
   Fletcher, Eric, 34
   Fletcher, Marianne, 29
   Galloway, Lyle, 33
   Horgos, William, 28, 106
   Hull, C.R., 30
   Jacobs, A. Douglas, 28
   Johnson, Melvin, 31
   Perry, William, 22-24
   Rosenfeld, Howie, 31
   Spring, Robert, 33, 106
   Vardeman, Judge Paul E., 34
   Wilson, Steve, 30, 106
   Yager, Rich, 15, 25-26, 27, 35, 106

Scrimshaw
    defined, 7-8
    durability of, 112
    old vs. new, defined, 22
    origin of word, 12-13
Scrimshaw, new
    crafted artifacts as, absence of, 35
    forged, 24, 28-30
    mass-produced, 24, 27-28
    materials for, 25-26, 29, 33, 38, 76-77
        passim, 111-12 (*see also* Ivory; Teeth)
    subjects for, 26, 35
        fantasy, 84-95
        miscellaneous, 76-83
        ships, 32, 57-75
        whaling, 22-23, 24, 26, 28, 42-47, 50
    techniques for making (*see* Techniques)
Scrimshaw, old
    crafted artifacts as, 8, 10, 12, 16
    crudeness of, explained, 18
    earliest extant, 9
    engraved, 8, 14-15, 16, 17, 18, 19
    materials used for, 8, 15-16, 17 (*see also*
        Teeth)
    subjects for, 14-15, 17, 19
    value of, 19, 24
Scrimshaw and Scrimshanders, 8, 29
Seaplay, the, on scrimshaw, 66
Selkirk, Alexander, 102
Serapis, the, 59, 61, 63
    on scrimshaw, 6, 62
Shickell, Jack, quoted, on last gam, 20-21
Ships
    pirate, 98, 102
    war, 54-56, 59-63 (*see also* names of indivi-
        dual ships)
    whaling, 5, 42-43, 46, 51 (*see also* Whalers;
        names of individual ships)
    wind, 53, 56, 57-73 (*see also* Windships;
        names of individual ships)
Ship models, prisoners make, 17
Ship models, scrimshander works from, 70-71
Sperm whale, 9-10, 11
Spring, Robert, 33, 106
Star of Alaska, the, ex *Balclutha,* 105
    ship, 56
    on scrimshaw, 107, 108, 109, 110, 111
Stephens, Dean, 32, 34
Susan, the, 18, 19
Susan's Teeth, the, 18, 19, 28
Techniques
    cracks, preventing and filling, 110-11
    design, drawing, 105
    engraving, 105-108, 109
    erasing, 107-108
    inking, 108-109
    mounting for display, 110

    polishing, final, 105
    sanding, 104-105
Teeth
    black market in, 38-39
    choice and preparation of, 104-105
    difficulty of obtaining, 19-20, 25
        (*see also* Legislation, restrictive)
    number of, in average whale, 12
    size of, 15-16
Tools, engraving, 105-106, 109
U.S. Naval Academy, 63
Vardeman, Judge Paul E., 34
Victory, H.M.S., 56, 59
    on scrimshaw, 54, 55, 70
Walrus ivory, 112
Wanderbird, the, on scrimshaw, 118
Wanderer, the, 22, 23
Warner, Abe, 4
Warships, 54-56, 59-63 (*see also names of
        individual ships*)
Wasa, the, 56, 59
    on scrimshaw, 65
Whalers, construction of, 51 (*see also names of
        individual ships*)
    equipment of, 5, 42-43, 46
Whales
    California gray, 46-47
    as endangered species, 36-39 (*see also* Legis-
        lation, restrictive)
    numbers of, killed yearly, 36
    sperm, 9-10, 11
        teeth of (*see* Teeth)
Whaling
    fatalities in, 36
    legislation restricting (*see* Legislation, res-
        trictive)
    modern methods of, 36
    origin of, 8-9
    a subject for scrimshaw, 17, 22, 23, 24, 26,
        28, 42-47, 50
    U.S.
        early, 9-10
        late, 16-17, 20-21
        moratorium on, 37, 39
Wilson, Steve, 30, 106
Windships
    a subject for new scrimshaw, 57-73
        depiction of, author's approach to, 70-
        71
        problems in reconstructing, 59, 61, 63
        (see also names of individual ships)
    surviving, 53, 56
Yager, Rick, 15, 27, 35, 106
    letter from, 25-26
Yankee Whaler, The, 8

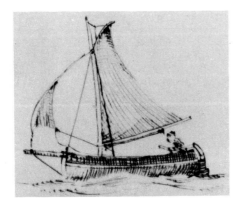